From the heart: this book is dedicated to my parents, Frank and Tess Reagan, and to my wife's parents, Jim and Phyllis Callan, for their constant support and love.

But it is especially dedicated to my wife, Carol. Our fifty-five years together were the happiest and most rewarding years of my life. There is no way I can put into words what those years meant to me and how fortunate I was to have her as the mother of my children. God blessed us in so many ways.

To my children and grandchildren: you have brought tremendous joy to our lives. I am proud of each and every one of you, and I am so grateful that you are so close to me, both in proximity and to my heart.

An Irish Prayer

*May God give you.....
For every storm, a rainbow,
For every tear, a smile,
For every care, a promise,
And a blessing in each trial.*

*For every problem life sends,
A faithful friend to share,
For every sigh, a sweet song,
And an answer for each prayer.*

Foreward

When you listen to someone's life experiences, a lot of things make sense.

Bob Reagan often acknowledges that he has had some lucky breaks in his life: a loving, supportive extended family; dedicated coaches, religious leaders, and various professionals who gave him chances and opened doors for him; a country that offered him a chance to go to college; character-building jobs and an opportunity to build a thriving dental practice; a community that provided leadership experiences.

However, it is what Bob *did with* these breaks that makes his story so remarkable. He has been grateful for each opportunity and has not taken his responsibilities lightly. As a son, serviceman, student, friend, husband, father, dentist, community member, and child of God, Bob has not been content with doing just enough to get by; it is in his character to go the extra mile.

After listening to Bob's story, it makes sense to me how so many people entrusted Bob with responsibilities and opportunities. I believe that they must have seen many promising characteristics in him: a strong work ethic, integrity, loyalty, earnestness, determination, sincerity, a love of learning, compassion, a positive attitude, and respect for others.

It has been such a privilege to compile this book. Throughout the process I often thought that the impact of Bob's life has had a ripple effect on so many people, and will continue to do so for generations to come. It is with great admiration that I present his story, and I am grateful that our paths have crossed. His mind and sense of humor are razor sharp. He is bold about his faith. He loves his children deeply and equally. He was devoted to his wife, Carol. He is a gentle soul and a faithful servant. His wise words ring true.

Passages in italics have been added to provide historical context.

Betty Kuperus Epperly
August 2012

Table of Contents

Irish Immigration to America

"The Gaels of Ireland are the men that God made mad, for all their wars are merry, and all their songs are sad." — G.K. Chesterton

Between 1845 and 1855 more than 1.5 million adults and children left Ireland to seek refuge in America. Most were desperately poor, and many were suffering from starvation and disease. They left because disease had devastated Ireland's potato crops, leaving millions without food. The Potato Famine killed more than one million people in five years and generated great bitterness and anger at the British for providing too little help to their Irish subjects.

Even before the famine, Ireland was a country of extreme poverty. A Frenchman named Gustave de Beaumont traveled the country in the 1830s and wrote about his travels. He compared the conditions of the Irish to those of "the Indian in his forest and the Negro in chains. . . . In all countries, . . . paupers may be discovered, but an entire nation of paupers is what was never seen until it was shown in Ireland."

Skibbereen 1847 by Cork artist James Mahony (1810–1879),
commissioned by *Illustrated London News*, 1847.

In most of Ireland, housing conditions were terrible. A census report in 1841 found that nearly half the families in rural areas lived in windowless mud cabins with no furniture other than a stool. Pigs slept with their owners and heaps of manure lay by the doors. Boys and girls married young, with no money or possessions.

A major cause of Irish poverty was that more and more people were competing for land. Ireland was not industrialized. The few industries that had been established were failing. The fisheries were undeveloped, and some fishermen could not even buy enough salt to preserve their catch. The agricultural industry was dysfunctional. Most large farms were owned by English Protestant gentry who collected rents and lived abroad.

By 1835, three quarters of Irish laborers had no regular employment of any kind. The only way that a laborer could live and support a family was to get a patch of land and grow potatoes.

Potatoes were unique in many ways. Large numbers of them could be grown on small plots of land. An acre and a half could provide a family of six with enough food for a year. Potatoes were nutritious and easy to cook, and they could be fed to pigs and cattle and fowl. And families did not need a plow to grow potatoes. All they needed was a spade, and they could grow potatoes in wet ground and on mountainsides where no other kinds of plants could be cultivated.

More than half of the Irish people depended on the potato as the main part of their diet, and almost 40 percent had a diet consisting almost entirely of potatoes, with some milk or fish as the only other source of nourishment. Potatoes could not be stored for more than a year. If the potato crop failed, there was nothing to replace it. In the years before 1845, many committees and commissions had issued reports on the state of Ireland, and all predicted disaster.

In the summer of 1845, the potato crop appeared to be flourishing. But when the main crop was harvested in October, there were signs of disease. Within a few days after they were dug up, the potatoes began to rot. Farmers were told to try drying the potatoes in ovens or to treat them with lime and salt or with chlorine gas. But nothing worked. In November, *a scientific commission reported that "one half of the actual potato crop of Ireland is either destroyed or remains in a state unfit for the food of man." By early spring of 1846, panic began to spread as food supplies disappeared. People ate anything they could find, including the leaves and bark of trees and even grass. Lord Monteagle reported to the House of Lords, people were eating food "from which so putrid and offensive an effluvia issued that in consuming it they were obliged to leave the doors and windows of their cabins open," and illnesses, including "fever from eating diseased potatoes," were beginning to spread.*

The blight did not go away. In 1846, the whole potato crop was wiped out. In 1847, a shortage of seeds led to fewer crops, as only about a quarter of the land was planted compared to the year before. The crop flourished, but not enough food was produced, and the famine continued. By this time, the mass emigration abroad had begun. The flight to America and Canada continued in 1848 when the blight struck again. In 1849, the famine was officially at an end, but suffering continued in the land.

More than 1 million people died between 1846 and 1851 as a result of the Potato Famine. Many of these died from starvation. Many more died from diseases that preyed on people weakened by loss of food. By 1847, the scourges of "famine fever," dysentery, and diarrhea began to wreak havoc. People streamed into towns, begging for food and crowding the workhouses and soup kitchens. The beggars and vagrants who took to the roads were infected with lice, which transmit both typhus and "relapsing fever."

Ireland had become part of Great Britain in 1801, and the British Parliament knew about the horrors being suffered. While the potato crop failed and most Irish were starving, many wealthy landlords who owned large farms had large crops of oats and grain that they were exporting to England. Meanwhile, the poor in Ireland could not afford to buy food and were starving. Many believe that large numbers of lives would have been saved if the British had banned exports and kept the crops in Ireland. The British government did take some steps to help the poor.

Image from Potato Famine Memorial in Dublin by Rowan Gillespie.

Before the famine, in 1838, the government had passed a Poor Law Act. It established 130 workhouses for the poor around the country, funded by taxes collected from local landlords and farmers.

Conditions in the workhouses were grim. Families lived in crowded and miserable conditions, and men were forced to work 10 hours a day cutting stone. Many people avoided workhouses if they could because moving in meant almost certain illness and likely death.

Parliament passed the Soup Kitchen Act in January 1847. The Soup Kitchen Act was intended to provide free food in soup kitchens sponsored by local relief committees and by charity. Free food was desperately needed. In July 1847, almost 3 million people were lining up to get a "vile soup" or a "stir-about" porridge consisting of Indian corn meal and rice. For most of the poor, this was the only food they had each day, and many were still dying of starvation.

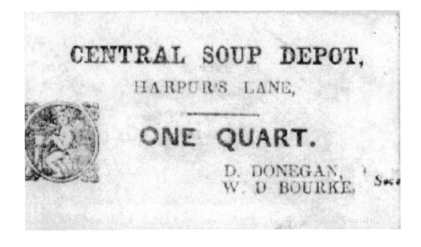

By September 1847, the local relief committees that operated the soup kitchens were almost bankrupt, and the government shut down the soup kitchens after only six months. With no more soup kitchens to feed starving people, little hope was left.

Driven by panic and desperation, a flood of emigrants left Ireland in 1847. Many left dressed in rags with not enough food to last the 40-day journey across the Atlantic and not enough money to buy food sold on board. Some went to Great Britain and to Australia, but most intended to go to America. Because fares on the Canadian ships were cheaper, many emigrants went by way of Canada and walked across the border into Maine and then south through New England.

The emigrants traveled on Canadian "timber" ships, which carried lumber from Canada to Europe and would otherwise have returned empty. The ship owners were happy to carry human ballast, but their ships were not equipped for passenger travel. The conditions on the timber ships were horrible. One philanthropist, named Stephen deVere, traveled as a steerage passenger in the spring of 1847 and described the suffering he saw:

"Hundreds of poor people, men, women and children of all ages, from the driveling idiot of ninety to the babe just born, huddled together without air, wallowing in filth and breathing a fetid atmosphere, sick in body, dispirited in heart, dying without voice of spiritual consolation, buried in the deep without the rites of the church."

Canadian ships became known as "coffin ships" because so many emigrants died during passage or after they reached land and were put into quarantine. Almost 30 percent of the 100,000 immigrants to Canada in 1847 died on the ships or during quarantine, and another 10,000 died on their way to the United States. Others who could afford the fare traveled directly to New York on American ships where conditions were much better. Some were already suffering from fever and were kept in quarantine on Staten Island.

Almost all of the Irish who immigrated to America were poor peasants from rural counties. Most were illiterate, and many spoke only Irish and could not understand English. The immigrants did not have the skills needed for large-scale farming in the American West. Instead, they settled in Boston, New York, and other cities on the East Coast.

Irish emigrants depart Liverpool for North America.
Pictorial Times - 1846

The men took whatever jobs they could find—loading ships at the docks, sweeping streets, cleaning stables. The women took jobs as servants to the rich or working in textile factories. Most stayed in slum tenements near the ports where they arrived and lived in basements and attics with no water, sanitation, or daylight. Many children took to begging, and men often spent what little money they had on alcohol.

The Irish immigrants were not well-liked and treated badly. The large number of new arrivals strained the cities' resources. Many unskilled workers feared being put out of work by Irish immigrants willing to work for less than the going rate.

The Irish also faced religious prejudice. With the large number of Irish immigrants, Catholicism was now the largest single Christian denomination in the country. Many Protestants feared that the Irish were under the power of the Pope and could never be truly patriotic Americans. As anti-Irish and anti-Catholic sentiment grew, newspaper advertisements for jobs and housing routinely ended with the statement: "No Irish need apply," as in this 1854 ad from the New York Times:

W. COLE, No. 8 Ann-st.

GROCERY CART AND HARNESS FOR SA
—In good order, and one chestnut horse, 8 years old
excellent saddle horse; can be ridden by a lady. Also,
young man wanted, from 16 to 18 years of age, able to wi
No Irish need apply. CLUFF & TUNIS, No. 270 W:
ington-st., corner of Myrtle-av., Brooklyn.

BILLIARD TABLE FOR SALE—Of Leona
manufacture; been used about nine months. Also,-
tures of a Bar-room. Inquire on the premises. No.

Because of discrimination, the Irish-Catholic immigrants tended to stay together in small "ghettos." They sought refuge in religion and began to donate to their local parishes to build schools and churches. But by 1860, with the advent of the Civil War, America's attention shifted to the issue of slavery, and discrimination against the Irish began to decline.

The "Know-Nothing Party," which was founded in the 1850s to prevent Irish immigration, lost all of its support. Large numbers of Irish Catholics who had enlisted in the Union Army and fought bravely came back from the war and found that things were beginning to change.

An Irish family arrives in New York City in 1929.

As America became more industrialized after the Civil War, Irish laborers found new, better-paid work. Many worked building railroads and in factories and mines. They helped organize trade unions and led strikes for shorter hours and better pay. And many became involved in local political machines and began to play a role in city and state politics.

The political machines, like Tammany Hall in New York, were associated with the Democratic Party and ran many of the big cities. In return for their political support, the Tammany Hall bosses helped immigrants through the naturalization process and even provided necessities like food and coal in time of emergency. The Irish Catholics ran Tammany Hall for years and helped many poor immigrant groups, including Poles, Italians, and Jews, as well as their own.

The Irish rose out of the ghetto not only because of politics, but also because of education. As the families of Irish immigrants became more prosperous, they were able to send their children to Catholic parochial schools run by the local parishes. After graduation from high school, many went on to college and then into careers in medicine, law, and business.

By 1900, only 15 percent of Irish-American men were still unskilled workers. By the 1920s, the Irish had spread into all spheres of American life. And in 1960, John Fitzgerald Kennedy, the great-grandson of a famine immigrant, was elected president of the United States.

Abraham Lincoln once said: "I happen temporarily to occupy this big White House. I am living witness that any one of your children may look to come here as my father's child has." The election of John Fitzgerald Kennedy as president in 1960 showed that the Irish Catholics had been assimilated into American culture and had left the misery of the Potato Famine behind them. Waves of other immigrants, fleeing poverty and persecution, have followed in their footsteps and slowly found acceptance, and success, in America. [1]

Reagan Roots

"When anyone asks me about the Irish character, I say look at the trees. Maimed, stark and misshapen, but ferociously tenacious." — Edna O'Brien

My father hit a dead end very early in his search to find details about his ancestry. He wrote to a family with the last name of O'Reagan in County Clare, Ireland, to inquire about a possible relationship connection. They replied, "Anyone who would drop the 'O' from O'Reagan does not deserve to hear from Ireland!"

All Irish surnames were originally prefixed with Mac or 'O'. Some families settling in Ireland from abroad even took on a name with a Mac prefix. This included the Vikings & the Normans. Some old Irish families would drop the Mac or 'O' during certain periods of turmoil, and this was also a common practice when the Irish emigrated to other countries.[2]

The Irish have a reputation for being very loyal and fun-loving, and I think that these characteristics are understandable if you consider their history. Ireland was oppressed, politically and religiously, for hundreds of years, and as a result they became more and more close-knit and proud.

Our ancestors were discriminated against because of their faith, so we cling to it more tightly. They had so little, but they learned to enjoy life, stuck close together, and invested in family and friends who were in the same situation. Their music, dancing and celebrations were an outlet and a form of expressing what they had undergone.

We do know that my great-grandfather, Michael Reagan, immigrated to Trenton, Ontario, in the late 1800s with his wife Bridget Conway Reagan. At that same time, other Reagans moved to Australia, which was a commonwealth country under the British crown. Earlier, in the 18th century, the British set up a prison colony in Australia and sent many Irishmen there as convicts when they fought for their independence.

Michael and Bridget Reagan had nine children, including my grandfather Dennis. The family moved to Kitchener, Michigan, in 1884 where they ran a general store. Dennis Reagan married Mary O'Dowd and became a streetcar conductor in downtown Grand Rapids.

When motorbuses started to replace streetcars, Grandpa Reagan refused to learn how to drive a bus. Since he had made some very wise real estate investments, he was able to retire early, in the 1930s. Grandpa Reagan also refused to own a car, so he and Grandma did not take trips unless someone else gave them a ride, and they walked everywhere from their home at 1029 Lafayette.

18

By the 1900s streetcars made urban life possible, and before the auto's momentum became unstoppable, streetcars were seen as essential for any city. Grand Rapids had its own distinguished streetcar history.

The city would experiment with a variety of streetcar types, including a steam driven car and a cable car line similar to the cable cars of San Francisco. By far the most important innovative period in Grand Rapids began in 1926 with the arrival of the Grand Rapids Electric Coach. For the next nine years Grand Rapids had the most modern streetcar system in the entire country until it was disbanded in 1935.

Grand Rapids was famous for personalizing its streetcars. The streetcar, the Spirit of St. Louis, was named in honor of a visit to Grand Rapids by Charles Lindberg. Even by 1920 automobiles were costing the streetcar company money and flashy streetcars were an easy way to advertise.

Another example of personalized streetcars was the Campfire Girls' car. This car was the counterpart to the Boy Scouts car, both of which were very popular. Scouts would stand at attention whenever the car rolled by.

Boy Scouts Streetcar, Grand Rapids, Michigan, 1926.

One of the most popular advertising techniques involved hiring young models to sit atop the cars with signs that read, "Don't worry, relax! Ride the streetcar; it's the safest place in town!"

Twenty-seven new streetcars brought out crowds on June 12, 1926, perhaps the grandest event in the city's entire streetcar history. Most people expected that streetcars would remain essential for all cities well into the future. The next week 50,000 people crowded into the West Michigan Fairgrounds to see the end of the old streetcars. Twenty old cars were primed with kerosene, hay, and black powder. While fireworks exploded into the air the cars were set ablaze. It was a symbolic gesture signifying the end of the old and the beginning of the new.

When the Great Depression began in 1929, money that was planned to support the streetcar network was diverted to other matters. After struggling for years, the Railway Company decided to abandon its fleet of streetcars and replace them entirely with buses. By the end of World War II nearly every major city in the country relied solely on buses for public transportation.[3]

Dennis and Mary Reagan had four sons: Francis (my father), Emmett, Edward and Leo. Emmett and his wife, Mary, lived in Grand Rapids until World War II, then moved to Chicago. Edward's first wife Sylvia died in childbirth; the baby girl survived and was given her mom's first name. Ed then married Alice Kubiak. Leo and his wife, May, moved to California.

Frank Reagan, 1922.

My father, Francis James Jerome Reagan, was born in August of 1900. Upon graduating from Catholic Central in 1918, he went to work for Doehler-Jarvis, which made aluminum die castings for automobiles.

In 1932 my father began to work for Goebel and Brown Sporting Goods, which turned out to be a job that would benefit our family in countless ways over the years. Goebel and Brown, co-owned by Paul Goebel and Thorne Brown, was located on 17 Library Street in downtown Grand Rapids, next to the YMCA.

Library Street, Grand Rapids, Michigan, circa 1945. Goebel and Brown is the second building from the right.

Both Goebel and Brown had played football and basketball at the University of Michigan, and were respected athletes in the community. Their store became the biggest sporting goods store in Grand Rapids, supplying all of the footballs and athletic equipment to schools in Grand Rapids as well as five other counties.

Paul Gordon Goebel (May 28, 1901 –
January 26, 1988) was an All-
American in 1921 at the University of
Michigan and the team's captain in
1922. He played professional football
from 1923 to 1926 with the
Columbus Tigers, Chicago Bears, and
New York Yankees.

After his football career ended, along with operating Goebel and Brown
Sporting Goods, he officiated football games for the Big Ten and served in
the U.S. Navy on an aircraft carrier in World War II. He was three times
elected mayor of Grand Rapids in the 1950s.

Goebel was friends with Gerald Ford's mother and stepfather and
recommended Ford to head football coach Harry Kipke at the University of
Michigan. When Ford returned from World War II, Goebel urged him to
run for U.S. Congress. Goebel was later the chairman of a committee
formed in 1960 to name Ford as the Republican Party's Vice Presidential
candidate on the ticket with Richard Nixon. [4]

My mother, Florence Theresa (Tess) Bowler Reagan, also had Irish roots. Her parents, Patrick Bowler and Elizabeth Farrell Bowler, settled in Parnell, Michigan, where they bought some land and had a small farm. My mother was born in August 1901 and had five sisters: Mary, Irene, Margaret, Gert, and Jane. The only Bowler son died at a young age, and

Tess Bowler Reagan, 1922.

because they had no sons to help with the farm work, the Bowlers decided to move to the city of Grand Rapids.

My mother was six years old when they made the move to 2242 Stafford Street in 1907. My grandfather, Patrick Bowler, became the custodian at St. Francis Church and School. When my mother was an adolescent, her mother (my Grandma Bowler) died of breast cancer. Grandpa Bowler died when I was a baby, also of cancer.

Patrick Bowler with his five daughters, 1922.

Early Years on Griggs

"You've got to do your own growing, no matter how tall your grandfather was." – Irish proverb

My parents, Frank and Tess Reagan, were married on Tuesday, August 12, 1924, at St. Francis Xavier Church. The reception was held at my mother's home. They paid $1500 for our first home at 543 Griggs in Grand Rapids. The house was quite small; it had two bedrooms, one bathroom, a small kitchen, and an attic.

This picture was taken the day I was brought home from the hospital.

I was born at Blodgett Hospital on February 16, 1926. My parents named me after Robert Emmet, an Irish statesman who led a rebellion against British rule in 1803. He was captured, tried, executed and beheaded at the age of twenty-two. Many Irish school children memorize "The Speech From the Dock," Emmet's last words on the eve of his execution, just as American school children memorize Abraham Lincoln's Gettysburg Address.

"A man in my situation, my lords, has not only to encounter the difficulties of fortune and the force of power over minds which it has corrupted or subjugated, but the difficulties of established prejudice: the man dies, but his memory lives."- Robert Emmet

When I was a young boy, much of our social life revolved around extended family and the parish. St. Francis Xavier was a tight-knit community, and we would all come together for various occasions: baptisms, 1st Holy Communions, weddings, and picnics. Mom's two sisters and their families, the Foxes and Longstreets, were within walking distance from our home. I spent a lot of time with these cousins and we thoroughly enjoyed our times together. The extended family had many reunions and we often put on skits. At most of the gatherings the beer was flowing, which guaranteed that there was always lots of storytelling and singing as well.

My sister, Mary Elizabeth, was born on November 11, 1928.

Since I was the first grandchild on the Reagan side, I received special treatment. For many summers I looked forward to spending a few weeks with my grandparents at their home on Lafayette. Their youngest son, Leo, was still home during some of my visits. Uncle Leo and I had a lot of fun together. His hobby was making gas-powered model airplanes. I was involved only minimally; I would have the honor of holding the plane as he glued on the parts. We would later try to fly these models, without much success.

A pear tree and an apple tree grew In my grandparents' backyard, as well as a beautiful garden. My grandmother and I would walk to Madison Square (Madison and Hall) for all of her shopping. She was a very small woman, and wore a red wig for many years. I was shocked when I found out that she had beautiful white hair underneath!

Their parish, St. Andrews, was ten blocks away. They were very devout, and we would walk to church every Sunday. Grandma Reagan was a tremendous cook, and she seemed to follow European habits in that she served meat and potatoes for breakfast. Lunch was a little lighter, and supper was the simplest meal of the day. My grandmother made the best sugar cookies in the world, and I could have as many as I could eat! Perhaps because I was so spoiled, I was never homesick.

I remember when I cut my finger on a new knife blade at their home. My grandparents put Sloan's Liniment on the fresh cut, which hurt more than the actual cut! My parents were upset when they heard how my wound had been treated, but my grandparents must not have had iodine, and Sloan's was their universal cure-all.

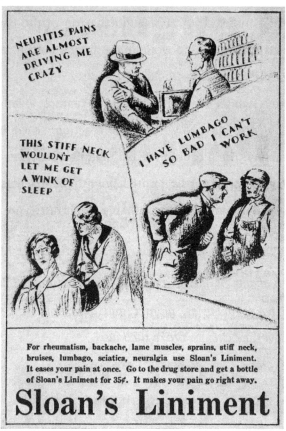

Sloan's Liniment contains capsaicin, the active ingredient in chili peppers that makes them hot. Capsaicin is used in medicated creams and lotions to relieve muscle or joint pain, but causes extreme pain if spread on open wounds.

Our little house on Griggs did have one feature that my dad appreciated: a basement, in which he manufactured home brew during Prohibition. My Uncle John manufactured the home brew, too. I have memories of people coming over -- not couples, just men -- and after a quick hello to us upon entering the front door, they'd go straight into the basement. When Dad designed his basement bar, he had included a special feature: a metal strip ran around the top of the bar, and when someone leaned against it, Dad would hit a hidden button. Whoever was leaning against the metal strip would get a shock.

The guys who knew of this special feature loved to bring in unsuspecting "victims" just to witness the reaction, so we had a steady stream of company. The alcohol that dad manufactured was supposed to ferment in a big vat for about six months, but I think they'd usually open it up after three or four months, so it probably didn't taste very good!

Prohibition was the period in United States history in which the manufacture and sale of intoxicating liquors was outlawed. It was a time characterized by speakeasies, glamor and gangsters, and in this time period many average citizens broke the law.

Temperence Movement poster, 1919.

After the American Revolution, drinking was on the rise. To combat this, a number of societies were organized as part of a new Temperance Movement, which attempted to dissuade people from becoming intoxicated. At first, these organizations pushed moderation, but after several decades, the movement's focus changed to complete prohibition of alcohol consumption. The Temperance Movement blamed alcohol for many of society's ills, especially crime and murder. Saloons, a social haven for men who lived in the still untamed West, were viewed by many, especially women, as a place of debauchery and evil.

Prohibition, members of the Temperance Movement urged, would stop husbands from spending all the family income on alcohol and prevent accidents in the workplace caused by workers who drank during lunch.

In 1919 the 18th Amendment to the U.S. Constitution, which prohibited the sale and manufacture of alcohol, was ratified. It went into effect on January 16, 1920. The Volstead Act clarified the law and stated that owning any item designed to manufacture alcohol was illegal. It set specific fines and jail sentences for violating Prohibition. The Volstead Act allowed alcohol consumption if it was prescribed by a doctor. Needless to say, large numbers of new prescriptions were written for alcohol.

A new breed of gangster arose during this period. These people took notice of high demand for alcohol and the limited avenues of supply. Al Capone from Chicago is one of the most famous gangsters of this time period. These gangsters would hire men to smuggle in rum from the

Caribbean (rumrunners) or hijack whiskey from Canada and bring it into the United States. Others would buy large quantities of liquor made in homemade stills. The gangsters would then open up secret bars (speakeasies)
for people to come in, drink, and socialize. As the perfect world promised by the Temperance movement failed to materialize, more people joined the fight to bring back liquor. The anti-Prohibition movement gained strength as the 1920s progressed.

Additionally, the Stock Market crash in 1929 and the beginning of the Great Depression started changing people's opinions. People needed jobs. The government needed money. Making alcohol legal again would open up new jobs for citizens and additional sales taxes for the government.

On December 5, 1933, the 21st Amendment to the U.S. Constitution was ratified. The 21st Amendment repealed the 18th Amendment, making alcohol once again legal. [5]

When I was 4½ years old I attended kindergarten at Dickinson Elementary School, a public school that was three blocks away from our home. For the next ten years I attended St. Francis Xavier School, which was six blocks away. At that time, we were still instructed by nuns and priests, unlike the Catholic schools of today.

Around 20 nuns lived in the St. Francis convent about two hundred yards from the school. The Sisters of Mercy had their hands full! The class sizes were 30-40 students, so the nuns had to be strict to keep order in the classroom. I was a pretty well-behaved student and did not give the nuns too much trouble, but I got my slaps every once in awhile. One time Sister Dorothy clubbed me right in the back of the head (I must have been talking to my neighbor) to get me refocused.

St Francis Xavier (a church of Spanish architecture), the Pastor's residence, and the school, circa 1930.

On May 28, 1933, when I was seven years old, I made my 1st Holy Communion. This day was both glorious and extremely sad at the same. The service was in the morning at St. Francis, and that afternoon, six family members and I rode in a cousin's 1933 Ford Coupe to get milk from the store. Four people sat in the front and three sat in the rumble seat in back, including my brother Gerald, who was twenty-two months old. Our car was hit broadside by another vehicle, and we rolled over three times. Gerald was killed. Although the rest of the family had broken bones, I was fortunate to escape injury.

My father was lucky during the Depression because he was still able to bring home wages at a time when many men lost their jobs. He earned $12 a week, and because we cut corners wherever we could, it was somehow enough to get by. We could not afford to keep our car, so my father took the bus to work.

America's future appeared to shine when Herbert Hoover was inaugurated President in 1929. However, soon the nation sustained the most ruinous business collapse in its history. The stock market crashed in the fall of 1929. On just one day, frantic traders sold off 16,400,000 shares of stock. At year's end, investors in the market had lost $40 billion. Banks failed, and millions of citizens suddenly had no savings. Factories locked their gates, shops were shuttered forever, and most remaining businesses struggled to survive. President Hoover and business leaders tried to convince the citizenry that recovery from the Great Depression was imminent. Farm prices dropped to record lows and bitter farmers tried to ward off foreclosers with pitchforks.

More than 4,340,000 Americans were out of work. More than eight million were on the street a year later. Wretched men, including veterans, looked for work, hawked apples on sidewalks, dined in soup kitchens, and passed the time in shantytowns dubbed "Hoovervilles." Starvation stalked the land, and a great drought ruined numerous farms, forcing mass migration.[6]

The church was a very important part of my upbringing. We had a block rosary group that took turns coming to each house once a week to say the rosary, and we spent time as a family in prayer as well. My father was president of the Holy Name Society for a year.

When St. Patrick's Day fell during Lent, which was often the case, a priest would come over to the parish and announce that, since it was St. Patrick's day, we did not have to fast. If St. Patrick's Day fell on a Friday, we could even have meat. We all gave up something for Lent as a form of penitence. Many adults gave up alcohol or smoking; I usually gave up candy.

I became an altar boy in the third grade, which I would continue to do through 10th grade. To be on the altar with the priest was a real privilege. We learned the Latin Mass and took some tests in order to qualify. At that time, masses were offered every day at 6:00 a.m. and 8:00 a.m.; St. Francis students attended the latter service on school days. Each month the altar boys would receive a schedule. We would be assigned to serve for a week's rotation every month during one of the masses.

In 1934 our family went to the World's Fair in Chicago. We took the train and stayed with my Aunt Margaret's family. Ironically, although we must have seen many amazing exhibits, the thing I remember most is going to see Sally Rand. I'm sure there were many more fascinating exhibits, but there was so much talk about Sally Rand, and I had never seen anything quite like her!

My dad and I stood in the back of the exhibit hall while Sally Rand was doing her striptease act. I was probably one of the few children in the audience. What sticks out in my mind is a flash of fabric. I think she had on layers of skirts, which she removed one by one, but I don't remember seeing anything revealing or shocking. I think it was the reaction of the crowd that made the biggest impression on me! There was lots of hooting and hollering. Afterwards, when my dad was taken to task by Aunt Marge and my mother for bringing me he said, "I don't think Bob could see anything!" I sort of went along with that.

The Chicago World's Fair opened on May 27, 1933, to commemorate the 100th anniversary of the incorporation of the City of Chicago and ran for two years. Its theme was to "attempt to demonstrate the nature and significance of scientific discoveries, the methods of achieving them, and the changes which their application has wrought in industry and in living conditions."

Some popular exhibits were the Midway (filled with nightclubs such as the Old Morocco) and a recreation of important scenes from Chicago's history. The fair contained exhibits that would seem shocking today, including offensive portrayals of African-Americans, a "Midget City" complete with "sixty Lilliputians" and an exhibition of incubators containing real babies. The first Major league All Stars Game was held at Comiskey Park.

One famous feature of the fair was the performances of fan dancer Sally Rand. Sally Rand had been a nightclub girl, and joined a chorus line at the fair. She was arrested for an "obscene" performance, and, as a result, was catapulted to fame. Her act grossed $6,000 per week during the depths of the Depression. Her signature performances were the ostrich feather fan dance and the balloon bubble dance.

One of the highlights was the arrival of the German airship Graf Zeppelin on October 26, 1933. For some Chicagoans, however, its appearance was not a welcome sight, as the ship  had become a prominent reminder of the ascendancy of Adolf Hitler to power earlier that same year.

Cadillac introduced its V-16 limousine, pictured here. Lincoln presented its  1936 rear-engined "concept car." The Packard, winning best of show, featured gold-plated hardware, burled elm paneling, and a dressing case which converted into a glass-topped table.

The Sky Ride ferried people across the lagoon in the center of the fair. It *had an 1,850-foot span and two 628-feet tall towers, making it the most prominent structure at the fair.   Suspended from the span, 215 feet above the ground, were rocket-shaped cars, each carrying 36 passengers.[7]*

Going to the movies was such a highlight of my childhood. Every other week we'd walk to one of three theaters that was close to our home: the Four Star Cinema, the Burton Cinema on Burton Heights, and the Madison at Madison Square. Movie tickets were a quarter in the 1930s. My favorite movies were westerns, and I loved anything with John Wayne or Tom Mix.

My parents were not really animal lovers. At one time we did have a Boston Terrier named Terry, I believe. Soon after we got it, it bit my dad's hand, and that was the end of Terry. My mom also had a canary named Tootsie for a long time.

In the summertime we often visited Aunt Dolly on her farm at the northeast corner of Pettis and Knapp in Ada. She and Uncle Paul had some cows, a few pigs, and some other animals. Their farm was within walking distance to the Grand River, so we would have picnics at the riverfront about once a month.

My mother's side of the family, including my cousins, would all get together at these picnics, and we always had a lot of fun. One of the highlights of these gatherings was the homemade ice cream, which was such a treat in the days before we had a refrigerator/freezer in our home! An advantage was, since we could not freeze any leftovers, we just had to eat it all, which meant second servings for everyone!

In the days before refrigerators we had an icebox, and every week we would pick up a big block of ice for a dollar or so at Consumers Power on Jefferson Street. We had a stand-alone freezer later, but families who could not afford one could rent freezer space at a special business.

Since freezers were not available to everyone, the soda fountain at the drug store was a popular hangout. There would be a counter in the back with stools and special booths for customers, and we could order soda, shakes and ice cream.

My dad's boss, Thorne Brown, gave our family a gift membership to the YMCA for a year. I took a few swimming lessons, but my instructor, after sensing that teaching me to swim would be quite a project, told me that some people are "born sinkers" who could not learn to swim. I'm sure he was joking, but I think he realized that he'd have to spend a lot of time with me in order for me to be successful, so I did not complete the course.

My grandfather had a brother in New Castle, Indiana. In the 1930s one of my uncles drove my grandparents and me to their home for a visit. That was the farthest away from home I had ever been, and it seemed to take forever to get there.

Our family also made a couple of trips to Detroit during the summers of my youth. We would stay with my Uncle Ed, who was a very vocal Union supporter. I remember that he liked to argue! He was also hard of hearing when it was convenient for him. As I have grown older I have realized that many men are selectively deaf.

My mother had a great sense of humor and was very quick to laugh. She loved to dress up and hosted plenty of parties at home. She belonged to the Bridge Circle, which was a group of about fifty women from St. Francis that would get together to play cards. The group even had a treasurer, and every time they played they would take a collection for church. As a family, we also played card games such as Setback, and although we may have played checkers, I do not recall playing any other board games.

Dad was very sociable, too. He and his brothers, my Uncle Ed and Uncle Norm, were big storytellers. They'd be in their element in our living room on Griggs, spinning their tall, outlandish tales. As I listened to them, I always wondered if they embellished, and I even piped up a few times to question the validity of the details. "Oh yes, that's the honest truth!" they would say. When I was a few years older and wiser I realized that not all of those stories were true.

There were only four homes on our block on Griggs. On one corner was a house in which my friend, Clyde, lived. He was an only child, and I remember that he had lots of toys; he had an amazing collection of toy soldiers and miniature cars. About once a month he'd let me come into his house and have the pleasure of playing with these treasures. My friend Joe Davis lived on the other corner, and, like me, he had lots of siblings but not many toys!

Our little house on Griggs became crowded quickly, especially after the twins, Patrick and Patricia, joined our household on August 23, 1934. My parents decided that it was time to move to a bigger house. The country was still suffering under the Depression at this time. Unbeknownst to us, we would soon experience economic relief, ironically because of the increased manufacturing and manpower necessitated by an event that would result in the loss of hundreds of thousands U.S. soldiers' lives: World War II.

Democrats nominated Franklin D. Roosevelt to run against Hoover in the 1932 election. His energetic, confident campaign rhetoric promoted something for "the forgotten man" — a "New Deal." Roosevelt went on to a decisive victory. In 1935 Congress enacted Social Security laws that provided pensions to the aged, benefit payments to dependent mothers, crippled children and blind people, and unemployment insurance. The election of 1936 triggered a nationwide endorsement of FDR.

Clamoring for their perceived share of the world`s pie, Germany, Italy and Japan marched onto the world stage. Germany came under the sway of Adolf Hitler and his National Socialist Party. Italy embraced Benito Mussolini's brand of fascism, and military rulers gripped Japan. The Axis powers began invade other countries.[6]

A Move to Willard

"I'm a firm believer in the theory that people only do their best at things they truly enjoy. It is difficult to excel at something you don't enjoy." - Jack Nicklaus

My parents paid $3000 for our home at 1922 Willard. It had two stories, with three bedrooms upstairs: one for my parents, one for Patrick and me, and one for Mary and Patricia. Although it was hard to say goodbye to our wonderful neighbors on Griggs Street, we found an equally welcoming group of people in our new neighborhood. One thing that we especially enjoyed was that we were very close to the park, which felt like our second home, especially in the summer. Again, we were within walking distance of St. Francis.

As a young boy I spent many hours drawing. My dad would bring home sporting goods magazines from Goebel and Brown, and I would look through them to find my subjects: fish, ducks and pheasants. However, I especially loved to draw airplanes. Eventually I designed wooden covers for the two scrapbooks that I kept for my drawings.

In school, I remember the nuns walking around the classroom and complimenting my drawings, which made me feel pretty proud. The poster that I drew for the school play was chosen as a display, and I think that once I drew a poster about saying the rosary. My cousin Gordy Fox, an artist himself, was very encouraging to me as well. I suppose it was my secret ambition for a while to be an artist.

I had areas in which I was not a star student as well! Although I was a "B" student generally, I was, and still am, challenged by spelling. Tom Zoellner and I were always the two worst spellers every year. We never improved. As a spelling bee would begin, all of the students would stand up and form a long line against the wall. When we misspelled a word we had to go back to our desk and sit down. Tom and I were always the first ones to sit down, and I think the nuns even felt sorry for us. One year they said, "We're going to do things differently. Today, you'll all start out sitting down. When you miss a word, you'll get to stand up." Of course, even in in this new arrangement Tom and I were the first ones to misspell a word, so when we stood up we felt no less conspicuous!

One of my favorite indoor activities was assembling model airplanes that were made from balsa wood and powered by rubber bands, but they never did fly very well! This was a common hobby. I think a lot of kids had dreams of becoming pilots.

Once a month or so I would buy a pack of Topps baseball cards for 1 or 2 cents. Included in the package was a piece of gum that tasted a little like cardboard.

As a grade school student, when I came home from school I did a little homework, and then I played outside until suppertime. In those days, our free time was unscheduled and unsupervised! The boys in the neighborhood would all get together and play sandlot baseball and football. In the winter we'd take our ice skates to the pond at Garfield Park and to the rink at St. Joseph's Seminary. This was another lucky break for me; since my dad worked at a sporting goods store, we had access to skates and other equipment.

Sometimes we would take our sleds to a hill at Eastern Avenue and Dickenson. One time I slid down and jumped off my sled, but another sled ran into me before I could get out of the way.

In those days, the blades on the sleds were straight, not curved like they are today, and one of the blades of the other boy's sled poked straight into my arm. I ran home and my mom patched me up.

One summer I built a scooter out of a wooden board and some old roller skates. It worked beautifully the first day, but the second day I hit a crack in the sidewalk, flew off, and broke my arm. That was the end of my scooter career.

Along with sports, I became interested in something else at about this time: girls. I had a crush on a girl when I was in sixth grade, but I never did tell the young lady about my feelings. I used to visit her quite often, and many times I took along a couple of buddies. At the school dances I had opportunities to ask her to dance, but mostly we just talked. It was pretty innocent.

Later on in middle school we would play "spin the bottle," but again, it never amounted to anything. We were never unsupervised, and there was always at least one parent nearby! I was more interested in sports than girls, and all of the sporting activities took up so much time that I stayed out of trouble.

Both of my parents had musical talent. My father was an excellent piano player, and even gave lessons in our home. Mother had studied piano seriously in school. You would think that with all of that musical ability, it would have rubbed off on the kids, but not one of us had a strong interest in the piano. I took lessons for a year, but my instructor told me that I should stick to baseball. I tried to play the violin, but it only lasted four months. Mary also tried the violin and lasted a little longer than I did, but she gave it up eventually, too. Our parents would play the piano and we would sit around and sing the popular songs of the time. The radio that we had in our home was not very fancy, but we put it to good use. Mother would listen faithfully to Bachelor's Children every day.

Bachelor's Children was a daytime soap opera that ran for over a decade, broadcast originally on Chicago's WGN in 1935, then syndicated nationally. Bachelor's Children follows the drama of Bob and his best friend, Sam Ryder, as the men fall in love with various women.

The series won Movie-Radio Guide's 1941 Award as "radio's best serial program," recognized as the "most representative script on the way of life of an average American family." [8]

On summer nights when the Detroit Tigers played baseball, I stayed very close to the radio. I was one of their biggest fans, and I pored over the sports section of the Grand Rapids Press, memorizing all of the players' statistics.

When I was eleven years old I joined a Little League baseball team through the American Legion. I was a pitcher, and like many other boys my age, I dreamed of becoming a professional baseball player.

When we won the Little League championship we were rewarded with the thrill of a lifetime. Our whole team went to a Detroit Tigers game in the summer of 1937, courtesy of Paul Goebel and Thorne Brown.

Along with a few other team members, I rode in a car driven by Thorne Brown. Traveling all the way to Detroit was a big deal! We sat in the stands by right field.

1937
DETROIT TIGERS

We went to a fancy restaurant after the game, and I ordered a pork chop. I couldn't believe my eyes when the plate was set in front of me. It looked about an inch thick! Even when I came home, I reported to my parents, "Well, the game was good, but you wouldn't believe the size of the pork chop I had at the restaurant!"

One of the families in our neighborhood had a bike. There were two girls in this family, and they did not have much of an interest in the bike, so I summoned up my courage and asked the mother if I could ride it. I'd ride that bike around the block about fifty times, happy as a clam.

When my cousin Ed offered to sell me his bike for $5.00, I considered myself very lucky – until the chain began to slip soon after I bought it. Ed's mom made him give me the $5.00 back, but I got to keep the bike. Even though it needed constant adjustments to the chain, at least it was mine!

When I was about twelve years old, I started playing golf with my parents. On summer days my friend Tom Zoellner and I would ride our bikes to a course near College and Michigan where we would play 9 holes for 25 cents. (The course has since been converted to a park.) Between the two of us we used three clubs and a few old golf balls, and although our equipment may not have been impressive, we had great times.

I was confirmed in the Catholic Church at the age of twelve. The nuns provided a list of saints' names, and I selected Leo, which became part of my official name, after my middle name.

When my dad had vacation time he usually just worked on projects around the house, especially during the years of the Depression when we did not have a car. Times were tough, but we always had necessities and were always a close family. Maybe because we were used to having so little and our expectations were low, my generation learned to be content. I never considered our family to be less fortunate at the time.

In 1939 when the economy improved, we purchased another car, and one of our first trips was to the Detroit Zoo. Sometimes during the summer we rented a cottage at Silver Lake or Big Star Lake for a week, which was a tradition that I would continue when I had my own family.

These days at the lake always provided enjoyable family time, even though I didn't swim. I don't remember seeing my parents swim, either; we just waded, but we still had fun.

My parents showed me the example of hard work, and they taught me to appreciate the work that you are given. My dad's job was not glamorous, but he thoroughly enjoyed his position, and he was thankful to have any kind of steady income, especially during the Depression. He made the best of his situation and was always positive. Starting in 1940, I remember traveling with my dad as far north as Newaygo, calling on various schools regarding their annual order for sporting equipment for their various teams.

Goebel and Brown staff, 1945. Thorne Brown and Paul Goebel are on the left; my father, Frank Reagan, is in front of them.

I also began to spend my Saturdays at Goebel and Brown, sweeping the floors and stocking shelves. Many high school coaches would visit the store and would meet in a special room in the basement. I think they might have even played cards!

Goebel and Brown built a nice new store at 12-14 Monroe, and my dad was promoted to manager. He really enjoyed every aspect of his job, especially helping customers select the right fishing tackle, baseball bats and gloves, etc. He retired in the 1960s at the age of sixty-five.

In 8th grade I began to earn a little extra income by taking on a paper route for the *Grand Rapids Press*. I had 100 customers on my Garfield Park route and made $1.85 per week. Those of us who had a route were told that we could deliver a 1940 calendar to our customers on New Years Eve. This was a big deal because it meant that our customers might actually give us a tip for our services. I could not believe my good fortune that night! Some customers would give a dime or quarter, some just said thank you, and others tipped me a couple of dollars. When I got home and counted that money, it was hard for me to fathom that I had collected $100, which was almost equivalent to a whole year's worth of wages! I went out and spent that money on a beautiful new bike at McGoverns on the corner of Division and Franklin and felt like the luckiest kid in town!

People were scared of polio during those years because we did not know how it was transmitted from one person to another. It seemed to be most contagious in the summer, so many of the moms kept their children away from pools and public places. My friend Tom Zoellner contracted polio and was at Sunshine Hospital, which used to be on Fuller Avenue, for almost a year. Although he had no lingering side effects, he was automatically exempted from service in WWII.

In the United States, the 1952 polio epidemic became the worst outbreak in the nation's history. Of the 58,000 cases reported that year, 3,145 died and 21,269 were left with mild to disabling paralysis.

Dr. Jonas Salk became a national hero when he developed the first safe and effective polio vaccine in 1955 with the support of the March of Dimes. Before the vaccine, the average number of polio cases in the U.S. was more than 45,000. By 1962, that number had dropped to 910. [9]

After 8th grade, half of our St. Francis class transferred to other high schools. Some went to South, the public school, and others went to Catholic Central. As a result, our St. Francis class size decreased dramatically in 9th and 10th grade. We were left with 9 boys and 15 girls.

Because of our small class size, we only had enough players for a six-man football team. Practice was every day after school until 6:00, so I would come home for supper and then do homework; there was not time for anything else. We played our games at Garfield Park, and were continually clobbered by the three other schools in the league, but we all got playing time and we thoroughly enjoyed ourselves. In two years we scored only six points, when I intercepted a pass and scored a touchdown.

On the evening of December 6, 1941, my parents were in a car accident; while they escaped injury, the car was totaled. The next day, on December 7, my sister Mary and I walked to the Burton Heights movie theater to take in a show. When we returned home my parents told us that Japan had bombed Pearl Harbor. We listened to the radio for more information, and I remember asking, "Where is Pearl Harbor?" It took awhile to figure that out; this event would effectively put Pearl Harbor on the map. At that time there were two newspapers that served the Grand Rapids area: the *Grand Rapids Press* and the *Grand Rapids Herald*, which was delivered in the morning. The Monday papers were filled with coverage about the bombing, and it was a couple of days before we realized how disastrous this would be for the United States, and how much our lives would change.

On December 7, 1941, the Japanese Navy launched a surprise attack on the United States, bombing warships and military targets in Pearl Harbor, Hawaii. More than 350 Japanese aircraft attacked the naval base in two waves, dropping armor-piercing bombs, and launching torpedoes toward U.S. battleships and cruisers. U.S. forces were unprepared, waking to the sounds of explosions and scrambling to defend themselves. The entire preemptive attack lasted only 90 minutes, and in that time, the Japanese sunk four battleships and two destroyers, pummeled 188 aircraft, and damaged even more buildings, ships and airplanes.

Some 2,400 Americans were killed in the attack; another 1,250 were injured. After the attack, Japan officially declared war on the United States. The next day President Roosevelt delivered his famous "infamy" speech and signed a formal declaration of war against the Empire of Japan. Within days, Nazi Germany and the Kingdom of Italy also declared war on the United States.[10]

In January 1942 the President called for unheard-of production goals: 60,000 warplanes, 45,000 tanks, 20,000 antiaircraft guns and 18 million tons of merchant shipping. Labor, farms, mines, factories, trading houses, communications — even cultural and educational institutions — were enlisted into the war effort. The nation generated new industries to mass

The U.S.S. Shaw explodes after being hit by bombs during the Japanese surprise attack on Pearl Harbor, Hawaii on December 7, 1941.

produce planes, ships, armored vehicles and numerous other items. Approximately 65 million men and women were in uniform or worked in war-related jobs by the end of 1943. Massive unemployment became a thing of the past. The Great Depression was swallowed up in the effort to defeat the Axis powers of Japan, Germany and Italy.[6]

In this generation most of the women were stay-at-home moms, but I think that World War II had a tremendous impact on the idea of women in the work force. During the war, women had to fill the factory jobs that were vacated by the men who enlisted. That's how they did their part. Women also found that they could add something to the family income. They paved the way for women of the future, and proved that women could be just as capable as men.

During World War II the United States government launched a propaganda campaign for women to support the war by taking on traditional men's jobs in factories and businesses. They invented the fictional character "Rosie the Riveter" to illustrate the ideal working woman: loyal, patriotic and efficient. The image of Rosie the Riveter became a cultural icon and is now used as a symbol to represent women's economic power.

I attended Catholic Central in 11th and 12th grades, from 1942-1944. For the first time in my life, I could not walk to school, and the bus trip to the high school cost 10 cents.

Catholic Central was quite a contrast to St. Francis. Our class at Catholic Central had 280 students compared to 24 at St. Francis. Another change was that boys and girls were taught separately; boys were taught in one building; girls were taught in a building across the street. Once again, I played football, but no longer on a six-man team! So many players on the Catholic Central team were better than me, so I was on the 3rd team. Some guys were built a lot different and had the muscular advantage, and I only weighed 138 pounds!

I worked my tail off in practice all week. We walked to Godfrey

Field, which was full of stones. I knew that, come game time, I'd be warming the bench, but I still enjoyed every minute of the experience! In my senior year, our team of thirty-seven won the Michigan State Championship!

We had only two choices of classes in high school. I took four years of Latin, four years of English, four years of math, four years of religion, one year of biology, and one year of general science. I was always pretty reluctant to ask questions in school. I felt uncomfortable standing up to talk, even when I was confident that I had the right answer!

The summer before my senior year I had a job in a factory that was within walking distance from our home. Two of my friends, Buckshot McCormick and Leo Hoban, also worked there. Our job was to put locks

1943 Michigan State Champions!
(I'm the last guy in the third row with the huge smile!)

together for Navy lockers. During my senior year I worked two nights a week at Cole's Laundry. Once in a while I'd help out my dad at Goebel and Brown, stocking shelves, running errands and sweeping.

In November of 1943 several of my Catholic Central classmates and I took some tests to qualify for either the Army or Naval Air Corp. I took both tests, but I was mostly interested in the Air Force. Air aces Hap Arnold and Colin Kelly were my heroes, and I aspired to be a pilot as well. The next month, in December 1943, my brother Michael was born. The boys' room would be even more crowded, but my family began to adjust to the reality that I might be leaving soon to enlist.

My brother, Pat, and I shoveling snow off the porch and roof at our home on Willard, 1943.

It took me many weeks to summon up the courage to ask a girl to the prom. I double dated with my friend Bill Brunner. His folks didn't have a car so we used my parents' car. I did not own a sport coat so I borrowed one from my cousin, Ed, who was in the service. I remember that we had a lot of fun at the prom, and it was probably one of the only times that I stayed out past midnight.

In early April I received a notice that unless I signed up for the Army Air Force by May 1, 1944, I would automatically be disqualified from this branch of service. I talked it over with the principal, Father Murphy, who said that I had enough credits to graduate, so I decided to enlist immediately. This meant that I would miss my graduation, but it was for a pretty good reason. At that time, most of us felt that it was an honor to serve. Our country was in danger, people were scared, and I was ready to be involved.

World War II Service

"I fear all we have done is awaken a sleeping giant and fill him with a terrible resolve." - Japanese Admiral Isoroku Yamamoto, upon learning of the success of the attack on Pearl Harbor.

I reported to Fort Sheridan, Illinois, on May 6, 1944. Although I had just left home, I applied for a weekend pass, and to my surprise, it was granted. I took the train home to Grand Rapids to celebrate Mothers Day.

After another week at Fort Sheridan I was sent to Sheppard Field in Wichita Falls, Texas. The Air Corps had all of the young men take classification tests, which determined our future roles. Instead of being designated for work as a pilot, I was appointed to train for the position of armored gunner. After basic training we left for Lowry Air Force Base #2 in Denver, Colorado, and arrived on July 21. The B-17 ball turret gunnery school took eight weeks, and I completed that course on September 7, 1944.

Several days before our graduation from this program, some buddies and I visited Lowry #1. A lieutenant stopped us and took down our names. We were afraid that we had done something wrong, but we soon found out that just the opposite was true, and this turned out to be another lucky break for me. At the graduation exercises our names were announced; we had been selected to go to CFC B-29 School at Lowry #1.

This was a terrific break, because it meant twelve more weeks in Denver, which was by far my favorite city during my service career! The courses were to prepare us to service the GE remote control turrets on a B-29 aircraft. We had every weekend off, so I was able to see all of Denver and the surrounding area.

The three other fellows who were selected with me became good friends and I have since had the opportunity to visit all three of them in their respective homes: Herb Newton in French Lick, Indiana, William Patrick in Memphis, Tennessee, and Tom Turner in San Francisco, California.

Newton, Patrick, Turner, Reagan: Denver, 1944.

Target practice, January 27, 1945: 148 hits out of 216 shots!

After we completed the training for operating the remote control turrets in Denver, we continued on to Fort Meyers, Florida, for gunnery school. We began by shooting .50 caliber machine guns from B-24s at moving targets pulled by women pilots. *(Operations manual used in WWII is pictured at left.)*

Women have served in military conflicts since the American Revolution, but WWII was the first time that women served in the United States military in an official capacity. Although women traditionally were excluded from military service and their participation in the Armed Forces was not promoted at the outset of World War II, it soon became apparent that their participation was necessary to win a total war. About 70% of women who served in the military during World War II held traditional "female" jobs such as typists, clerks, and mail sorters.

Women served in unique branches of service: the Women's Army Auxiliary Corps (WAC), the Women Air Force Service Pilots (WASP), and the Women Accepted for Volunteer Military Service (WAVES). Women also served in the Marines and in a branch of the Coast Guard called SPARS (Semper Paratus Always Ready). Although women's jobs may have been less glorified than those of the men fighting on the front lines, women were essential in maintaining the bureaucratic mechanisms that are necessary in total warfare. Also, by filling office jobs that would otherwise be held by men, women freed more men to fight. Women were not permitted to participate in armed conflict but their duties often drew them close to the front lines. One way that women participated in work

that put them in danger was through their services in the Army and Navy medical corps. [11]

After completing this most exciting part of my training I received my first leave to go home, and I arrived home on March 15, just in time to celebrate St. Patrick's Day. After the week at home I continued to Lincoln, Nebraska. Here we were assigned to crews, and I was assigned to the 6th Bomb Group Association and sent to Tuscon, Arizona, to the Davis Monthan Field. After only three days we had our first flight on a B-29!

It was necessary to first become acclimated to taking off and landing in the B-29. We repeated this process for six hours, all the time practicing shooting at targets on the ground.

The left and right gunners got really sick on the first flight. I was in the top gunner position and managed to keep from turning green. The tail gunner, Johnny Quadros, and I became very close friends, and we remained close while we were overseas. Altogether we flew 120 hours to complete our training. Of all the airfields in which I was stationed, Davis was by far the best. Besides having the best food, we really felt like we were being well prepared for overseas action!

Before we went overseas we had training for various scenarios. One event that sticks out in my mind is when we went out to the dock. We were supposed to jump in the water so that we could learn to respond to water-related situations. Since I had never learned how to swim, I told the instructor that if I jumped in the water I'd hang on to the edge of the dock and would not let go. Furthermore, I told him that if he pushed me off I'd come back to haunt him for the rest of his life. He ended up letting me pass without going through the water exercises, which probably wasn't wise.

However, I knew that if we parachuted in the water we would be equipped with a Mae West vest, which would inflate before you hit the water when you engaged a little cartridge. *(The aircrew called their yellow inflatable, vest-like life preserver jackets "Mae Wests" partly from rhyming slang for "breasts" and "life vest" and partly because of the resemblance to the torso of Mae West, a popular starlet of the times.)* I knew that life preserver would be my safety net if I ever got close to the water!

From Tuscon we went to San Francisco for a couple of days and then we flew to Hawaii. After a couple more days we flew to Guam, and then finally to Tinian, which would be our home from August 1945 to April 1946. The islands of Guam and Tinian are a part of the Mariana Islands, an arc-shaped archipelago made up by the summits of fifteen volcanic mountains in the northwestern Pacific Ocean.

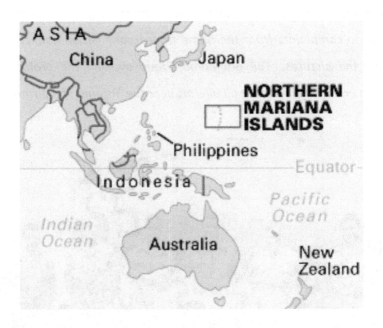

The 6th Bomb Group included the 24th, 39th and the 40th squadrons. Each squadron included air crews, ground crews and other service personnel. Each had their own separate tasks to perform in completing the missions assigned to the Group. In accordance with Air Force tradition, each squadron had an official insignia. When the 6th Bomb Group aircraft first entered service in February, they did not have a lot of decoration. A name might be stenciled on the side and the rudder might have the oldrudder markings. By the end of the war, all of the aircraft had the "Circle R" on the rudder.

Almost all crews gave nicknames to their airplanes. Initially, the nicknames were just painted on the side. Later, the crews also began to *decorate their aircraft with artwork, often of scantily-clad women. In response to complaints from the home front, many Group commanders censored the pictures. The 6th Bomb Group avoided the problem by issuing an order requiring that all aircraft bear the insignia of a pirate.*[12]

6th Bomb Group. Back Row: Goldman, Gratix, Vincent, Fraking, Rosenblatt, Ray. Front Row: McKim, Miller, Quadros, Reagan.

Back home, my mom and other homemakers did their part to economize, and many items were rationed by the government because they were needed in the war effort: gasoline, tires, sugar, meat, silk, shoes, and nylon.

Even though I enjoyed most of the routine of the Air Corps, there were aspects that I did not enjoy, but I believe it is important to focus on

The U.S. Government encouraged rationing with a variety of posters.

the positives. Even Kitchen Patrol (KP) was an educational experience! The lower ranks were a little envious of the officers when we saw some of the benefits they received. For example, the enlisted men received two (warm) beers per week, but the officers got a fifth of whiskey, for which they only paid $1.85.

Although the 6th Bomb Group was not called on to be involved in active combat, the island of Tinian would soon become famous throughout the world because the atom bombs, Little Boy and Fat Man, were dropped on Hiroshima and Nagasaki from planes that were launched from the island of Tinian. The reason that Tinian was chosen for this mission was due to its proximity to Japan and because it was long enough to accommodate the necessary airstrip.

Aerial view of Tinian.

In late July of 1945 the *SS Indianapolis*, the Navy's fastest destroyer, brought supplies for the bombs to Tinian from San Francisco. From there the *SS Indianapolis* continued toward the Philippines, but a Japanese submarine torpedoed the ship on July 30, 1945. The *Indianapolis* sank within minutes.

Over 300 men went down with the ship, and the remaining 900 men faced exposure, dehydration and shark attacks as they waited for assistance while floating with few lifeboats and almost no food or water. The Navy learned of the sinking when survivors were spotted four days later by the crew of a PV-1 Ventura on routine patrol. Only about 300 sailors survived. This was the greatest single loss of life at sea in the history of the U.S. Navy.

Although the atom bombs were to be launched from Tinian, my group (the 6th Bomb Group) was not informed about these plans for obvious security reasons. The Manhattan Project (the program that produced the first atom bomb) was so secretive, and we had no idea that the United States possessed the technology to construct atom bombs.

The 509th Composite Group, which was assigned the duty of dropping the atom bombs, was completely separated from us from the minute they arrived on Tinian until August 15. They had orders not to communicate with us, of course. Now we know that they were isolated for a reason.

While their airplanes were parked along with ours, the crew members of the 509th were very well guarded. We were envious of them because we suspected that they were planning something special. One tip-off was that the area in which they loaded the bomb was unique. A ditch had to be dug because the bomb was so big, and they had to drive the B-29 over the ditch to load it. The atom bombs barely fit in the bomb bays on the underside of the plane.

The 509th Composite Group was created in September 1944 when Major General Leslie Groves, the man in charge of the Manhattan Project to construct the atomic bomb, foresaw the need for a dedicated corps of men trained to drop the bomb on Japan. He chose twenty-nine-year-old Lieutenant Colonel Paul Tibbets to command the group. Groves provided Tibbets with fifteen Boeing Superfortresses and eighteen hundred men, and ordered him to shape them into a self-contained, secret outfit.

If Tibbets ran into any bureaucratic problems, he needed only to mention the code word "Silverplate," which revealed nothing about the group's mission, but magically cut through red tape. If thwarted nevertheless, he had direct access to Groves and, if need be, to H. H. "Hap" Arnold, commanding general of the Army Air Forces. Tibbets's top secret mission was to forge a group to deliver an atomic bomb to Japan and survive. For this he had to devise the means and train his crews to drop this incredibly powerful bomb and escape before its terrible blast could consume them.

The next few weeks were spent on practice runs. On July 12 the aircraft participated in a raid on Marcus Island, fully loaded with seven thousand gallons of fuel and twenty 500-pound bombs, weighing the maximum sixty-seven tons on takeoff. Like all the other 509th heavy bombardment air crews, Lewis and his men were required to fly half a dozen missions to prepare for battle conditions and their ultimate mission.

Tibbets made time to fly on some of these practice missions. But he was under strict orders not to go along on the flights over Japan. He knew too much for the United States to risk his capture. The group knew their mission was special; they knew the maneuvers they would have to carry out; but they knew little else. The 509 was comprised of 15 specially configured B29 "Flying Fortresses". By Sunday, August 5, 1945, everything was ready. The clouds that had hung over Japan's home islands for a week were clearing. Tomorrow would be the day.

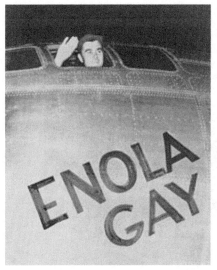

Aircraft 44-86292 had not yet been named. Tibbets got a painter to brush "ENOLA GAY" in bold black capitals just below the pilot's window on the aircraft's port side. It was his mother's maiden name and Paul Tibbets' way of honoring her for standing by his side in an often rocky early career. (This photo was taken prior to takeoff on August 6, 1945.)

Just after noon that Sunday, the bomb--nicknamed Little Boy, in spite of its ten-foot-length and four-and-a-half-ton weight--was removed from its heavily guarded assembly hut on Tinian's North Field and loaded into the modified bomb bay. That evening the seven crews taking part in the mission gathered for the preflight briefing shortly after supper. Later, at 11:00 P.M., the crews of the Enola Gay and the two planes that would accompany her to her target received a final briefing. This was the first time they were told the expected power of the bomb they would drop.

Takeoff took place at 2:45 A.M. on August 6, 1945. Tibbets held the aircraft at low altitude while Captain Parsons crawled back to arm the bomb. When they reached Iwo Jima, they circled the island to let the other two airplanes catch up, and with them on his wings, he gradually climbed to higher altitude.

The 509th Composite Group on Tinian with an assembly of military and technical personnel before the bombing of Hiroshima.

They had a seventeen-hundred-mile trip ahead to Hiroshima and the crew took turns napping. This would be a thirteen-hour round-trip mission, and for a while there was little to do. As the Enola Gay approached the city, the crew could clearly see it from more than fifty miles away. As the bomb dropped, the aircraft jumped, relieved of its weight, and Tibbets went into his sharp turn. Forty-three seconds later, as the bomb reached detonation altitude preset at 1,890 feet above ground, the sky lit up.

Even with dark goggles over the crew's eyes, they felt as though someone had sparked a flashbulb in their eyes. The shock wave arrived another forty-five seconds later. This was the moment of truth. The aircraft rocked, but withstood the blast. The immediate danger was over.

Meanwhile, the mushroom cloud was rising faster than anything any of them had ever seen, soon reaching an altitude of nine miles, three miles above their own cruising altitude. A soldier on the ground was quoted as saying it "looked like a pot of bubbling tar." However, despite the tremendous damage that resulted from the bomb, the Hiroshima mission did not end the war.

The Hiroshima mission's bomb (Little Boy) was cigar-shaped, like most bombs. It derived its explosive power from uranium. It weighed 9,700 pounds, was 10 feet long and 28 inches in diameter.

In contrast, the explosive for the bomb dropped on Nagasaki was plutonium, an element that does not exist naturally on Earth.

Fat Boy had to be manufactured from uranium 238 in giant nuclear reactors in Hartford, Washington. It weighed 10,213 pounds, was 10.7 feet in length and 5 feet in diameter.

Tibbets decided not to go on the second bombing mission himself, and assigned the command to Chuck Sweeney. Since Sweeney's plane (The Great Artiste) had been outfitted for instrumentation, he was assigned to fly Bockscar, while Fred Bock, who normally piloted the plane that bore his name, would command the instrumentation aircraft on this flight.

The Nagasaki mission was plagued with troubles. A faulty fuel pump prevented complete use of the fuel on board. Kokura, the primary target for the mission, was so overcast that Sweeney had to give up after circling the city for some time. The alternate target, Nagasaki, was also heavily overcast, but Sweeney did drop the bomb. Then, heading home, he was so low on fuel that he had to land on Okinawa to refuel before proceeding back to Tinian.[13]

Every flight group had its own tail insignia. The 6th Bomb Group's identifier was the Circle R, and the insignia of the 509th, which flew the A-bombs, was a circle with an arrow. For this one mission, however, the Enola Gay was painted with the Circle R so as not to attract additional suspicion from the Japanese.

After the first bomb was dropped on August 6, 1945, the guards left, and some of the 509th Group mingled with us. We were just as surprised as the rest of the world, but it was quite exciting to be closely tied to such an historic event. That was before the days of television, of course, but we saw film footage of the atom bombs being dropped, and we knew that this would likely be the end of the war.

Japan surrendered on August 15, and on Tinian we celebrated with the rest of America. There were hugs and cheers, and the level of excitement was incredibly high. I was thrilled especially for the guys who had been on Tinian since January and completed their thirty-five missions; their exuberance was genuine and heartfelt because of what they had been through.

At this time there was a shift in focus for the soldiers. It became necessary to concentrate on relief efforts for the many prisoners of war (POWs). The majority of POWs were put to work in mines, fields, shipyards and factories on a diet of about 600 calories a day. Prisoners were continuously hungry, and many were skin and bones when they were rescued. When the Japanese finally surrendered, the prison guards and officials abandoned the camps, leaving prisoners to fend for themselves.

The 6th Bomb Group dropped supplies over a POW camp in Funatsu, Japan, on September 8, 1945. These supplies were tied to wooden platforms, attached to parachutes and released from the bombbays. We encountered a problem on our mission. The shroud lines became tangled in the bomb bay doors, and the doors would not close.

Our pilot, Captain George Vincent, told me to go into the bomb bays and cut the tangled lines. Somehow I managed to creep along the bomb racks and cut the lines loose, which allowed the door to close. The mission was a success; we were able to drop the supplies! These missions were rewarding because we felt we were doing something positive. Of course, since the threat of attack did not exist, these missions also resulted in fewer air crew and aircraft casualties.

CFC Gunner Robert E. Reagan and 1st Lieutenant Don Ray, Flight Engineer, filling the left wing tank in Iwo Jima after dropping off supplies for POW camp in Funatsu, Japan, on September 8, 1945. The return flight to Tinian would take fourteen hours.

Captain George Vincent, Johnny Quadros and I flew more flights than other crew members. As a result, I received three promotions, reaching the rank of Technical Sergeant. I was proud, yet humbled, to receive the stripes. There was only one higher enlisted rank (Master Sergeant) but achieving this would have required an additional two months of service, and I was eager to return to Michigan.

The wings on my uniform identified my position (gunner) and rank (technical sergeant). The ribbons represented good conduct, and battle stars indicated our activity in the Asia Pacific. Along with my uniform, I also kept a shell from a .50 caliber machine gun.

My parents were both very faithful letter writers, so I received a steady stream of news from home. After the Allied victory was assured, these letters were no longer censored. One day my parents sent me a telegram, a rare occurrence: my brother Thomas was born on December 28, 1945. This news was quite a surprise, as I did not even know that my mother was expecting! With his arrival, the boys' bedroom at home would become quite crowded; now there would be four of us.

1945 DEC 30 AM 7 02

PO53 GRANDRAPIDSMICH 24/23 1155AM 29TH
LT TSSGT BOB REAGAN 36468359 39TH
BOMBING SQUADRON 6TH BOMBING GROUP APO 336 GUAM

NEW BROTHER ARRIVED DECEMBER 28 ALL WELL XX

FRANK REAGAN

It was time to refocus and think about what it would be like to return to civilian life. I realized that being able to fly in a B-29 as part of the crew had been such an honor. At the age of only eighteen I had been given the opportunity to travel to so many different parts of the country and meet some wonderful guys along the way, which is something I will never forget.

Part of the 6th Bomb Group, including Johnny Quadros, was transferred to Clark Field in the Phillipines on February 2, 1946. In March the rest of us received orders that we would be returning home. Instead of going directly home, we were first sent to Saipan, another Mariana island. Due to typhoons and other delays, we stayed there for six weeks.

We finally boarded a ship on April 4. After arriving in the United States on April 16, we took a train to Camp McCoy in Wisconsin where the final discharge from service took place. Fort McCoy was used primarily for training missions for groups that were preparing to enter combat during the war, but it had also been used as a POW camp. After stopping in Milwaukee, we took a $25 flight to Grand Rapids. When we arrived in my hometown I caught a bus home.

Subject   Quadros, Date
Vincent, Reagan

My parents were surprised when I showed up in full uniform in the doorway, as they did not know exactly when I would be coming home. The night I returned, Dr. Fred Rickle, a dentist, just happened to be visiting my folks. After my family and I exchanged hugs and shed a few tears, Dr. Rickle asked me what I was going to do with my GI Bill of Rights. I didn't have the slightest idea, and he suggested that I pursue dentistry. I was open to suggestions, and that sounded pretty good to me. I have often joked that if an undertaker had been visiting my dad the night I returned home, that could have been my career!

Getting My Feet Back on the Ground

"Never in the field of human conflict was so much owed by so many to so few."-
Winston Churchill

Now that I was home, it was back to reality. Being in the service made everyone grow up twice as fast. When WWII veterans came back from service, they were welcomed back with open arms. We felt like we had contributed to something very important, and we were thrilled that we had survived!

The Frank Reagan family, 1948.

Veterans were all able to participate in the government-sponsored 52/20 Club: for 52 weeks, all veterans could go in and collect $20 every week. I collected the money for four or five weeks, but I started to feel like I was taking advantage of a handout, so I began looking for work. I took on many odd jobs before my college plans were a sure thing.

My first job, for which I was paid $1.50 an hour, was painting high-tension towers around Grand Rapids. On the first day the foreman handed me a bucket of paint and a brush and told me to climb up the framework and start painting. Not only were the towers extremely tall, we were not provided any safety harnesses. I was never so scared in my whole life! I painted for three hours and never looked down; my legs were shaking the entire time. Then I dropped a can of paint, and my imagination got the better of me. I realized that I could be next, so I climbed down and told the foreman that I would not be back the next day.

The working conditions in my next job were comparatively tame and better paying, but the downside was that it was a little boring. At Fox Deluxe Brewery my job was to keep the truck drivers supplied with products that they were to deliver to their customers. In the middle of the summer the brewery closed. It was time for another change.

During my next job at General Motors, I worked harder than I had in my entire life. It was an incredibly hot summer, and I don't believe the thermometer ever dipped below 90 degrees. My job was to place a thin steel plate in the wheel well of the trunk floor. A trunk would come along on the assembly line every ten seconds, so I had to work fast! Because the blades were sharp, I would wear out a pair of gloves every few days. From my station on the line, the trunk would move along and plate was welded in place, and on it would go. Some of the workers had been doing the same job on the line for five years, and I developed tremendous respect for them. At the same time, the experience made me even more determined to get to college.

Even though I knew it was shot in the dark, I still had a dream of becoming a professional baseball player. That summer the New York Yankees held tryouts at Bigelow Field in Grand Rapids. I decided to give it a try, but when I arrived at the field I was so nervous I could hardly talk! The first day consisted of testing our prowess in the outfield; balls were hit to us, and I must have done okay, because I was asked to come back the next day.

On the second day we had batting practice. I knew the catcher, and he told me that he had called for a fastball, but I still missed. In the end, the scouts and coaches determined that I could field, throw and run pretty well – but I couldn't hit. So I put that dream behind me and went on to pursue something more practical.

I am very thankful that I was able to attend college. Once I finally got there, I was motivated to study hard because I had known firsthand the challenges of the working class. Although my parents had not attended college themselves, they were very supportive of me and helped out as much as they could. Another lucky break for me, as well as for countless other veterans, was the G.I. Bill of Rights.

Our country was willing to give back by providing veterans with an education. This was such a tremendous bonus. Several of my cousins who had also served in the war did not take advantage of these provisions of the Bill of Rights. They had solid jobs before the war (three of them with Michigan Bell), and these jobs were waiting for them when they returned home. I was young enough to fully benefit from these provisions, and a college education made the whole experience worthwhile for me.

The GI Bill of Rights, known as The Servicemen's Readjustment Act of 1944, was signed into law on June 22, 1944, by President Franklin D. Roosevelt. The major force behind the bill was the American Legion, a veterans advocacy group founded in 1919. It labeled the resulting ideas, "a bill of rights for GI Joe and GI Jane." The term GI stood for "Government Issue," referring to military equipment. The adoption of the bill was not merely the result of generosity on the part of a grateful Congress. It was also a product of fear about a radicalized postwar America.

Prior to WWII, America had provided benefits and care to those disabled by combat, but paid little attention to able-bodied veterans. Neglect of WWI veterans had led to protest marches and disastrous confrontations. In 1932 20,000 veterans gathered in Washington, D.C. for a "bonus march," hoping to obtain financial rewards they thought they had been promised for service in WWI. President Hoover called out the army, which under General Douglas MacArthur and Majors Dwight Eisenhower and George Patton used guns and tanks against the "bonus army." The GI Bill was enormously democratic. Benefits were available to every veteran who had served at least 90 days and received an honorable discharge. Few *people were aware of the implications of this revolutionary new law. Commentary tended to stress the benefits of the unemployment allowance and to underestimate the education and loan program provisions. The readjustment allowance authorized $20 a week of unemployment funds for 52 weeks — and soon became known to its beneficiaries as the "52-20 Club."*

Because of the Great Depression, few in the age group of GIs had ever held a job. Skeptics said that the giveaway of $20 a week would lead to irresponsible idleness. Opposition arose in Congress from southern members who resisted providing that much money to blacks. Yet — and this is indicative of that generation's response to the war's end, and the stigma in those days that came with accepting public money — only half the veterans even claimed the money; most used it only for a few weeks. For educational benefits, the VA paid tuition, fees, and books, and provided a monthly living stipend. For home loans, the VA guaranteed a portion of the loan to the lending institution at a low 4 percent interest.

Among the legacies of the GI Bill is the belief that education can be available to anyone, regardless of age, sex, race or religion. Millions of vets had not even graduated from grammar school. Only 23% had a high school diploma and 3% had college degrees. Few colleges were prepared for the numbers of veterans who reg-

istered for classes. Many major universities doubled or tripled their enrollments. Campuses sprouted makeshift dormitories, prefabricated huts for classrooms, and even trailer camps. It is estimated that approximately half of the 16,000,000 WWII veterans took advantage of this provision to receive a college education.

These graduates raised expectations throughout the country, and their skilled labor contributed to a literate middle class. There was no going back to the old America dominated by farming and small towns. By the early 1970s, one in five Americans had a college education, compared to one in 16 prior to the war.

The GI Bill was one force leading to enormous social change. Views regarding sex, religion, and race were shaken up. It led to a great mixing of different groups on campus. About 64,000 women veterans of World War II took advantage of the bill's education opportunities. Jewish veterans gained entry into many schools previously known to reject Jewish applicants. Many black veterans were turned away from overly crowded black institutions and yet could not attend white southern schools. It took several years to accomplish what the GI Bill could not. During the 16 years of depression and war, it was not just the lack of new housing, but also that existing homes had fallen into disrepair.

After World War II building resumed, but materials were in short supply. By the end of 1947, the VA guaranteed over one million loans for homes *and businesses. Under the VA Loan, the government co-signed half of a veteran's mortgage. This encouraged developers to build and bankers to lend, often with no down payment.*

What the GI Bill represented is that a national commitment to mobility pays dividends for both individuals and the nation. The GI Bill enabled the nation to overcome instability, restored human, economic, and social capital, and helped catapult the U.S. to leadership on the world's stage.[14]

I attended Grand Rapids Junior College (J.C.) for $60 a term and completed the pre-dental program in two years. Living at home allowed me to save some money, and for two days a week I worked at the Wyoming Yard of the C & O Railroad. At that time the U.S. Post Office hired part time seasonal carriers, and for three years I delivered mail at Christmastime. My route was in the area of Eastern and Franklin.

I had the opportunity to work for so many businesses, and I was grateful for every experience. Now I was ready to concentrate on a new future and looked forward to a career in dentistry.

My sister Mary married Jim Gire in 1951. Jim's Polish ancestors' original last name was "Gerowicz" (although I am not sure of the correct spelling). Jim had two brothers, and after their father passed away they decided that they would legally replace their Polish surname with a more pronounceable Americanized name. Ironically, they could not agree on a way to spell the replacement. Jim selected the name Gire, one brother chose Gyre, and the third brother went with Geier.

Back row: Frank and Tess Reagan, Mary and her fiancé Jim Gire, me and Patrick. Front row: Michael, Grandma Mary Reagan, Thomas, Grandpa Dennis Reagan, and Patricia.

Dental School at Marquette

"The mediocre teacher tells. The good teacher explains. The superior teacher demonstrates. The great teacher inspires." — William Arthur Ward

I had applied to the School of Dentistry at Marquette University in Wisconsin. As it turns out, since many other soldiers were applying for colleges at the same time, the competition was stiff. In 1947-1949 about 1500 students applied for dental school, and only 100 were accepted each year. I was thrilled when a letter arrived to tell me that I was one of the lucky future students. The letter from Marquette stated, "It was only through the efforts of Dr. Bill VerMuelen and Dr. Fred Rickle that you (Bob Reagan) were accepted at Marquette."

Having the endorsement of those two dentists was one of the luckiest breaks of my life! I learned that sometimes it's not *what* you know, but *who* you know!

Tuition was considerably higher at Marquette ($500/term) than at J.C.; I learned so much and had extremely interesting classes, but I had to work hard. Similar to when I was a grade school student, it was not too often that I would raise my hand to volunteer an answer. The difference here was that we had some professors who reveled in their position of power and enjoyed intimidating the students. This was their way of motivating us to do the assigned studying the night before. Two classmates passed out from fear when they did not know an answer!

One of these professors taught pharmacology, and after the second student fainted he must have felt terrible because he gave us a long, heartfelt talk. He was such a kind old man, and assured us that it was okay if we did not know all the answers.

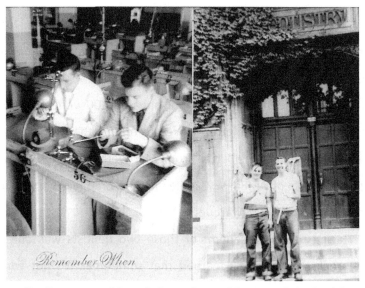

Jim Bouressa and I worked together on Marquette's janitorial staff while we were classmates.

The other professor, however, an oral surgeon, scared the living daylights out of us and never apologized. Once, while we were observing an extraction, he handed the forceps to a student, and that was enough to make the boy keel over and faint. The professor didn't miss a beat; he ignored the fainter and handed the forceps to someone else.

Finally, Father McEvoy (Regent of the Dental School) intervened and told the professors to let up a little bit because fear was not an effective motivator, and then things did change for the better. The program at Marquette was light on theory but heavy on practical experience, and I felt that I received a very thorough education.

Our first two years at Marquette were primarily spent in the laboratory, although we had a class in the morning and another in the afternoon. During our freshman year, training included the dissection of a cadaver.

Best buddies at Marquette Dental School: Jim VandeWalle, Robert Reagan, and Jim Bouressa, pictured at an A.D.A. Convention.

The cadavers were never women, only men, and were probably homeless derelicts that were not claimed by family members. Four or five students were assigned to each cadaver.

We started at the head, and spent most of the time here, as this had the greatest relevance to our profession. Then we continued to the neck, the chest, and the abdomen. We may have dissected just one arm and one leg. Our instructors felt that it was important for us to have a general knowledge of the anatomy of the entire human body, as evidence of problems with the teeth and gums can be indicative of other underlying health problems.

It was in 1947 that I voted in the Presidential election for the first time. I voted for Harry S. Truman, who won the election in a big upset over Dewey. My entire family was strong Democrats, and many of my dental friends were Republican. I have usually voted Republican, but on several occasions I have voted for a good Democrat.

As a presidential candidate, Gov. Thomas Dewey of New York was stiff and tended toward pomposity. "The only man who could strut sitting down" was the crack that made the rounds. But on November 2, Election Day, the polls and the pundits left no room for doubt: Dewey was going to defeat President Harry S. Truman. And the Tribune would be the first to report it.

Arguably the most famous headline in the newspaper's 150-year history, DEWEY DEFEATS TRUMAN is every publisher's nightmare on every election night. Like most newspapers, the Tribune, which had dismissed him on its editorial page as a "nincompoop," was lulled into a false sense of security by polls that repeatedly predicted a Dewey victory. Critically important, though, was a printers' strike, which forced the paper to go to press hours before it normally would.

As the first-edition deadline approached, managing editor J. Loy "Pat" Maloney had to make the headline call, although many East Coast tallies were not yet in. Maloney banked on the track record of Arthur Sears Henning, the paper's Washington correspondent. Henning said Dewey would win the election. The ink was hardly dry on 150,000 copies of the paper when radio bulletins reported that the race was surprisingly close. The headline was changed to DEMOCRATS MAKE SWEEP OF STATE OFFICES for the second edition. Truman went on to take Illinois and much of the Midwest in this whopping election surprise.

Truman, traveling by rail to Washington two days later, stepped to the rear platform of the train in St. Louis and was handed a copy of the Tribune early edition. He held the paper up, and photographers preserved the moment for history.[15]

Love at First Sight

"Love begins by taking care of the closest ones - the ones at home. It is not how much we do... but how much love we put in that action." - Mother Teresa

My cousin, Mary Louise Benham, was also a student at Marquette University. She often tried to set me up on a blind date with a girl whose name was Carol Ellen Callan. I always had an excuse, though. I was content to be single and I was so shy around girls. Studying and working took up all of my time, and besides, I didn't have any extra money to spend on dates. However, I could not make excuses forever, and as fate would have it, Carol and I were destined to meet.

Mary Benham was married on June 30, 1951, on the west side of Grand Rapids. At the reception my Aunt Dolly played the part of cupid and said, "Bob, I want you to meet one of the bridesmaids. This is Carol Callan." Our polite how-do-you-do was not enough for Aunt Dolly. She said, "Come on, Bob, give her a little kiss!" After I gave Carol a peck on the cheek, Aunt Dolly pushed for me to give her a bigger kiss, so I did. I'm sure

Carol was just as embarrassed as I was. Later in the evening I asked Carol to dance. We hit it off right away, and it truly was love at first sight. I was immediately impressed by her good looks and her pleasant and happy attitude. We exchanged addresses and telephone numbers, and she returned to Milwaukee.

Since I knew I would be traveling to Milwaukee in September, I thought I would just look her up then, but Carol set me straight. Three weeks after Mary's wedding I received the most blistering letter in which she reprimanded me for not corresponding with her. Apparently I needed some lessons in the etiquette of romance!

Carol and I dated during our junior year and it did not take us long for us to figure out that we wanted to be married. I asked her father for her hand in marriage and then popped the big question at park in Milwaukee. Although she was my first and only serious girlfriend, Carol had been pursued and proposed to by various boyfriends, but I was the lucky guy to whom she finally said "yes!"

My folks were thrilled; Carol was the nicest girl in the world! I also got along very well with her folks. Her father and I played a lot of golf together. I helped him around the house, and he let me use their car whenever I needed it. I had the best in-laws in the world!

Carol's paternal grandfather, Christopher J. Callan, was born in 1845 in Dublin, Ireland. After immigrating to the United States he married Mary Ellen Whalen Callan. They lived in Grandville, Michigan, and had seven children including Carol's father, James Jay Callan. James Callan served in the U.S. Navy during World War I, and after the war he settled in Milwaukee, Wisconsin, with his wife, Phyllis Pieplow Callan. The German heritage and influence in the Milwaukee area is widespread; Phyllis' parents, Charles and Barbara Pieplow, were of German descent and lived forty miles south of Milwaukee in Elkhorn, Wisconsin.

While in Milwaukee, James Callan worked as a representative for Ford Motor Company. His job was to present the new lines of automobile models to Ford dealerships. However, during World War II, car sales were down because so many men were in the service and gasoline was rationed, so he then sold war bonds.

This involved going to businesses and convincing people that purchasing war bonds would support the military and would also benefit them personally, because they would be supporting the war effort in the United States. War bonds came in many different denominations; for example, the face value may have been $10, and it could be redeemed for $25 when it matured after a certain period of time. My folks had bought a couple for me during the war, as they did for all of my siblings.

Carol and I wanted to get married in December of 1952, but her folks suggested that we wait a little longer, and we took their advice. I married the love of my life on February 14, 1953, at St. Anne's Church in Milwaukee, Wisconsin. Getting married on Valentines Day helped me to always remember our anniversary.

Mr. and Mrs. James J. Callan
request the honour of your presence
at the uniting of their daughter

Carol Ellen
with
Mr. Robert E. Reagan

in the
Holy Sacrament of Matrimony
on Saturday, the fourteenth of February
at ten o'clock in the morning
St. Anne's Church
N. 36th and W. Wright Streets
Milwaukee, Wisconsin

RECEPTION FROM 2 TO 5 P. M.
HUBBARD LODGE
3565 N. MORRIS BOULEVARD

We were given the choice of getting married on February 14 (the last Saturday before Lent) or getting married after Lent, as the Catholic Church did not allow weddings during Lent at that time. We were married by Father Farrell, who was Carol's first cousin on her father's side and my second cousin on my mother's side. Carol's folks gave us a choice: their gift to us would be either $500 or a reception after the wedding ceremony, and we chose the reception.

Our wedding was not huge, and we both had about the same number of guests. My family and friends came from Grand Rapids and Chicago and Carol's were from Milwaukee. I did not own a dark suit, so I borrowed one from Gerry Knape, a dental classmate who remained a good friend until his death in 1994. Our reception was at Hubbard Lodge.

Our honeymoon destination was a surprise to Carol. I made reservations at the Palmer House in Chicago for three nights. I was so glad that some people gave us cash for wedding gifts, because I needed it all to pay for the train trip and the hotel bill! I returned to dental school on Tuesday, and as I took my place in the classroom I really took a lot of ragging from my classmates!

Our first home, which we rented for $62 per month, was a small apartment in Milwaukee on 28th street near the Eagle's Lodge off Wisconsin Avenue. Besides taking classes, I did assorted odd jobs and earned about $25 per week. For three years I worked as the janitor for the dental school. I also worked as a hospital orderly and did some janitorial work at Wisconsin Bell Telephone Company. The best job I had during my time at Marquette was at the Pabst Blue Ribbon Brewery between my junior and senior year; I received $2.00 an hour.

Since Carol and I lived on a shoestring budget, we gratefully accepted offers from her family when they invited us over for some wonderful home cooked meals.

I graduated from Marquette in June of 1953. Although the difficult work of studying and finals were behind me, the grueling work of taking the Dental Boards was still ahead of me.

I took the Wisconsin Boards at Marquette and the Michigan Boards at the University of Michigan. Each began on a Monday morning at 8:00 and finished on Friday afternoon. Those were the two longest and toughest weeks of my life. There was lots of tension in those exam rooms, because we all knew that if we did not pass, we would not receive our license to practice. The questions and procedures covered everything that we had learned during our four years of dental school. We had to make a denture, an amalgam filling, an inlay and a bridge. We also had to provide our own patients on which to perform these procedures! We did not receive our results until July 15, and it was with great relief that I found out that I had passed!

Settling Down in Lowell

"Blessed are they who hold lively conversations with the helplessly mute, for they shall be called dentists." — Ann Landers

My dad was still working for Goebel and Brown Sporting Goods at this time, and one of his customers, Dr. Shepard, told my dad that the town of Lowell could use another dentist. Although Lowell was only twenty miles from Grand Rapids, I had only been there once in my life. L.B. Bignall, a man who owned a dental supply company, accompanied me to look at some property that was for sale. It seemed like a suitable office, and I decided that Lowell would be a good place to live and work.

Carol and I rented a little apartment in Lowell at the corner of Washington and King. I started my practice on July 22, 1953, with one patient. My office was on Main Street over Christianson's Drug Store, overlooking the Flat River. There were many other practices and professionals in the same building who would become my colleagues and mentors: Dr. Shepard MD, Dr. Hill MD, and the accounting offices of

Abrahams & McMahon, DAs.

Getting involved in Lowell was easy because the people were so friendly, and we were soon invited to join a euchre club. There were nine couples in the group, and every three weeks or so we'd get together to play at one of our homes. The host couple would set up four card tables and have the honor of serving while the other sixteen people played cards.

Carol finished her nursing program in September of 1953. Very soon she would have the opportunity to care for her first tiny "patient": our first daughter, Jane Ellen, was born on November 22, 1953, nine months and eight days after our wedding!

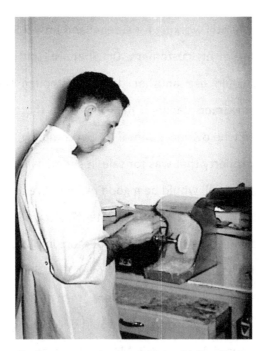

Dr. Reagan works on a lathe, which polishes dentures and crowns.

Carol was a natural mother, and she loved babies. We rejoiced when, less than a year later, Karen Elizabeth joined our family on October 25, 1954. We soon outgrew our little apartment! The month after Karen was born we moved into our first home at 1027 Vergennes, a three-bedroom ranch. We paid $11,500 and our monthly payments were $81.25. The extra space was appreciated but we did not realize how soon we would outgrow this home as well!

We bought our first black and white television set in 1954, the year after we moved to our home. I bought it at a shop that was kitty corner from my office. The technology had not been perfected, so when I had some problems with the TV, the store from which I bought it claimed that they could not help me, and I had to find a specialist technician.

When I got the television fixed I looked forward to watching, for the first time, Notre Dame University play a live football game. I had settled in with the television on when my cousin came in unexpectedly from Detroit. I hadn't seen this cousin in a couple of years, but this was Notre Dame football! I tried not to be impolite, but I kept glancing at the screen. My cousin could not have cared less about the game, and he did not get my hints! There would be plenty of other sporting events-football, baseball, golf, etc. that I would be able to enjoy in the future. We bought our first color TV to watch the Detroit Tigers participate in the 1968 pennant race. It was a thrill to watch them win the World Series!

As a family, we watched some variety shows that were popular at that time, such as Milton Berle and Ed Sullivan. We had so much going on in the house with lots of little folks running around that needed attention, so television was not a very big part of our lives.

Television struggled to become a national mass media in the 1950s, and became a cultural force in the 1960s.

Many critics have dubbed the 1950s as the Golden Age of Television. As the households with TVs multiplied, more varied programming came in. Situation comedies and variety shows were formats that were borrowed from radio. Former vaudeville stars like Milton Berle, Sid Caesar and Jackie Gleason found stardom after years of toiling on the stages.

During the 50s, quiz shows became popular until a scandal erupted. For three years, producers of "The $64,000 Question" supplied an appealing contestant with the answers to tough trivia questions to heighten the drama.

In the 1950s and 60s, television news produced perhaps some of its finest performances. Edward R. Murrow exposed the tactics of innuendo and unsubstantiated charges that Sen. Joseph McCarthy used to exploit the country's fear of Communism. The televised debates between Kennedy and Nixon were credited with giving JFK a slim election victory. Filmed coverage of the civil rights movement and live coverage of Martin Luther

King's March on Washington brought those issues into sharp focus. When President Kennedy was assassinated on Friday, November 22, 1963, most Americans immediately turned on television sets to get the news. The networks devoted days and days of airtime to coverage of the tragedy, the funeral and the aftermath. Many Americans (who may have come home from church early) were watching live coverage on Sunday morning November 24, when they saw Jack Ruby kill the alleged assassin Lee Harvey Oswald.

Later, coverage of the Vietnam War was credited with, for the first time, bringing war into the living rooms of citizens. When CBS News anchorman Walter Cronkite editorialized against the war, President Johnson was reported to have said, "If I've lost Cronkite, I've lost the country."

Yet, this was also a time of abundant escapism on television. Producers added science fiction to the mix of genres on TV, perhaps in response to the NASA space program. This era produced some of the most enduring reruns in the history of television. "Star Trek" is the prime example.

In the midst of the turmoil of the 60s, the most popular shows were set in a rural past that was disappearing. In the 1960s the "Andy Griffith Show" stayed in the top ten every year, reaching number one in 1967. "Petticoat Junction" (1963-70) and "Green Acres" (1965-71) both proved to be popular. CBS decided it needed to attract a more youthful Baby Boomer audience, and began to produce such shows as "The Mary Tyler Moore Show," All in the Family and M*A*S*H in the 1970s.

All in the Family revolved around the lives of the Bunkers, a working class family Queens, New York. The show broke ground in its depiction of issues previously considered unsuitable for U.S. comedy, such as racism and breast cancer. The show ranked number-one in the Nielsen ratings from 1971 to 1976.

M*A*S*H (1972 to 1983) followed a team of doctors at the "4077th Mobile Army Surgical Hospital" in South Korea, during the Korean War. It struggled in its first season and was at risk of being cancelled. In Season two it aired after All in the Family, and it became one of the top 10 shows of the year.[16]

A friend of mine who was a classmate during my years at J.C., Jim Gollner, became a Paulist priest. Carol and I went to New York City for his ordination in 1954. When he passed away in 1984 I was asked to give the eulogy.

Another classmate, Robert Hesse, became a Holy Cross priest after graduating from Notre Dame with a degree in engineering. He served in Uganda, Africa, his whole life. After every three years of service, he would come home in the summer, and I did his dental work during his sabbaticals. His body had difficulty adjusting to the American diet when he returned, as the diet in Uganda is heavily dependent on rice and other foods that are indigenous to the area. On his last leave, Father Hesse told me that it would be the last time I would see him, and his words were accurate; he passed away in 2007 after a long life of service.

Rev. Fr. Robert Hesse, CSC (RIP)
1926 - 2007

When I started my practice people did not have dental insurance, so when the choice was to save the tooth for $100 or take it out for $25,

90% of my patients would opt for removing the tooth. My parents had dentures, as did most people of that generation, because procedures that involved saving the teeth were costly. The Teamsters Union offered insurance in 1954, and General Motors and other companies soon followed, which changed treatment options dramatically.

Grand Rapids was the first city in the United States to fluoridate water. Dr. Doug Oatley and I served on a committee to decide if Lowell should follow. An opposition group appeared before the committee and claimed that if we fluoridated water, we would be forcing people to drink poison. We did not see any evidence to support this claim, so the committee made the decision to begin fluoridating water in 1954.

Scientists first began noticing the effects of fluoride on teeth in the early 1900s when a Colorado dentist discovered that some of his patients had very few cavities and it was traced to a water supply naturally high in fluoride. Fluorides are chemical compounds that occur naturally in both soil and water. In the 1930s, studies found that one part per million— roughly one droplet in a bathtub full of water—would prevent cavities without causing mottled enamel. In January 1945, the City of Grand Rapids was the first community to add fluoride to a public water supply. [17]

In 1955 Dr. Oatley, who had practiced in Lowell for twenty-one years, moved to Calumet, Michigan. I bought some of his equipment and moved my office to 207 West Main Street.

207 West Main Street, Dr. Robert E. Reagan, D.D.S .

Shortly after I opened my new office I attended a seminar in Big Rapids on nitrous oxide (i.e. "laughing gas"). The fellow I went with told me that he had attended the seminar several times, but he just could not make the decision to use it in his office. Well, I put it right in my office the next week. For me, it was all about the comfort of my patients; if the patient is relaxed, so is the dentist.

I did not hesitate to add this improvement because I understood the level of fear that some people have for the dentist, especially men! Men are the biggest cowards when it comes to pain. If I had 50 difficult patients, 40 of them were men. I firmly believe that if men had babies, there would only be one child per family.

I am so thankful that Carol did not have that problem. We were thrilled when another healthy, beautiful girl was added to our family. Kathleen Elaine was born on September 8, 1956. Our house on Vergennes was feeling a little crowded with three little folks....and another one soon on the way, so in February 1957 we moved to 427 King Street in Lowell. We paid $20,500 for the two-story house, and our monthly payments were $132 for 15 years at 5½% interest. On October 22, 1957, we welcomed our first son, James Edward. Mary Eileen joined our growing brood on March 12, 1959.

I had lots of fun as an endman for the Lowell Showboat from 1959-1961. There were six of us, three on each side of the stage, and one by one we would come out to the microphone, tell a corny joke or two, and demonstrate a little (very little!) talent. One guy played the trumpet, others sang, and I did a little soft shoe dance. We performed in blackface, common at the time, but of course that would be frowned upon these days.

Although Carol and I hoped to have many children, we could not have anticipated how greatly the Lord would bless us. Margaret (Peggy) Erin was born on August 13, 1960. Since Carol's middle name was Ellen and mine was Emmett, we gave the first six children a middle name that started with an "E," but we ran out of suitable options after Peggy was born. Ruth Ann was born on December 14, 1962, and Patricia (Patty) Marie joined the family on April 29, 1965.

Our last two children were boys: Donald Charles, born on March 3, 1967, and Edward John, born on October 22, 1968. That made ten children for us. It became more of a challenge each year to get the kids to pose for our annual Christmas card picture. Carol's brother John and his wife Mary Ann had eleven kids, so the Callans had twenty-one grandchildren!

Our 1960 Christmas photograph.

Over the years we made many improvements to the house on King Street. It became a challenge to figure out sleeping arrangements in our four bedrooms at times, but we made it work. One year our home was on a special Historic Home Tour; people could buy a ticket and walk through our home, as well as others in town. We stationed the kids in different rooms, and when people came through the kids would give a little rundown about the room. The kids got lots of use out of the playroom, and the sunroom was where we displayed all of our Irish paraphernalia, a collection that seemed to grow every year.

The sunroom also became the home for my first dental chair when it had to be replaced by a newer model in my office. Because the chair was so elevated, the kids just loved it. (Patty now lives in the home with her seven children, and it seems that no matter when I visit, the chair is occupied!)

The kitchen in this home had a built-in icebox, which we used as a linen closet because we already had a refrigerator. I built a deck, and in 1973 we installed the first hot tub in Lowell. That was the closest Carol came to kicking me out of the house. Installing the hot tub required the removal of three beautiful windows and replacing them with a sliding glass door, which, Carol knew, would make it very difficult to keep the room warm in the winter. But I think she forgave me because she ended up enjoying the hot tub immensely!

I had been inspired by the relaxing hot tubs at the ski resorts out West. Our hot tub was about four feet in diameter and six feet tall, so we had to use a ladder to climb in! The tub was made from cypress wood and was actually a sawed-off recycled vinegar vat that I purchased from the Kellogg Vinegar Plant in Lowell. After several years I installed a hot tub that bore more of a resemblance to the designs that are common today.

As our household expanded over the years, so did my practice. Along with keeping up with a steady stream of patients, it was necessary to be knowledgeable about new techniques and equipment. As dental students, we had done all of our work on patients while we were standing up because the patients sat upright.

Standing up over the patient was very tiring, and many dentists developed back problems. Dentists performed procedures with a mirror, which of course requires you to do the opposite of what you see, so this took some practice in order to be proficient.

Shortly after I began to practice, it became common for patients to recline in the chair, so dentists could sit down as well and put the mirrors away. We also began to use carbide rather than steel burs on drills because they last much longer. We went to composite fillings as opposed to silicates, which needed to be replaced much more often.

Silver (amalgam) fillings have always been cheaper, but these became less popular over time. Handpieces (i.e. drills) began to be powered by compressed air, which afforded an amazing increase in speed, from 4500 revolutions per minute to 200,000 per minute.

The 1960s were years of transition for the dentist. Advancements which began to occur at this time would have occurred about ten years earlier if it were not for WWII. During the war, there were many advances in science and technology, which helped win the war. In peacetime these would have been translated into progress to benefit professions such as medicine and dentistry. After the war, many of these advances were channeled into the private sector.

During the first sixty years of the 20th century, dental students were taught by professionals who were taught in the late 19th or early 20th centuries. After the war a new generation of dentists came on the scene with new ideas, materials and concepts. Many of these resulted in the development of new techniques, medicines, instruments and equipment.

A young dentist starting out in the early 1960s found himself in a new era of sterility. Previously, dentists sterilized their needles and instruments by placing them in boiling water. Disposable needles were first used during WWII. Besides this, the use of an autoclave increased. Cold sterilization became commonplace, which replaced the concept that most dental instruments only had to be as clean as knives and forks.

High-speed drills were introduced in the late 1950s. Some dentists obtained belt-driven high-speed drills and others air-driven high-speed drills, which they usually attached to their units. High-speed drills and the water coolants that accompanied them brought about changes in equipment, as well as office design.

At first, portable suction units were either attached to the dental units or were next to them in mobile cases. When high-speed drills with attached water coolants became available, many dentists were more comfortable working in a sitting position, although many dentists continued to work standing up.

Many dentists also realized that it was more comfortable for them to work sitting down, rather than standing up, with the patient in a reclining position.

In the early 1960s, new safer x-ray machines, with better radiation protection and electronic timers, were replacing the older machines. With the introduction of new impression materials, such as rubber base, indirect procedures became commonplace. The era of the dentist constructing gold inlays and crowns in his office laboratory was coming to an end as these procedures were taken over by commercial laboratories. Dentists could now take impressions, send them to a laboratory, have the restorations made and insert them.

As for operative dentistry - amalgams, gold inlays and silicate fillings were for the most part still the norm. When preparing amalgam, excess mercury was removed by the use of a squeeze cloth. Silicate fillings were known to last on average only three to four years. Although acrylic filling materials were available, it would be several years before the concept of bonding, composite filling materials and bonded composite fillings would become the standard.

The age of specialty began to take hold in the 1960s. Although general dentists still practiced oral surgery, endodontia, and periodontia, many now referred cases to specialists in the fields. Many general dentists continued treating children, but pediatric dentistry became a popular specialty. With the increased number of specialists, the quality of dentistry being practiced in America continued to increase.[18]

Part of the stress in dentistry comes from knowing how people feel about being in the chair. With every patient you're a little tense, hoping and praying that whatever you do does not hurt them, yet it's important to convey to the patient that they are in good hands. At least once a day, a patient would say to me, "You don't know how I've dreaded this appointment."

I tried not to carry that stress home with me; playing golf was an outlet and a way for me to let off steam and find peace.

Still, going to the office was something I looked forward to every day. I enjoyed helping people and the various challenges that came with running a practice. (*Of course I dressed professionally, but I made an occasional exception, as you can see here!*)

As I was building my practice at the office, Carol was just as busy at home. I don't know how she did it, but being a mother and running a household was very natural for Carol. As our kids got old enough, they went to school at St. Mary's in Lowell. Four nuns came from Ireland to teach and lasted about five years.

One day, while I was painting the convent, Father Strahan invited me to become involved in the Serra Club of Grand Rapids, an organization that supports young boys as they consider a life of service in the priesthood.

Under Father Speer Strahan, plans that had begun by Father John Grzybowski were completed and St Mary's Parish built its school for $120,000.00 in 1952. In its first year of operation it had 44 students who were taught by Dominican nuns from Ireland. These were followed by Dominicans from Marywood. On January 24, 1963, St. Mary's paid off the school's debt, and Father Strahan served until his death in 1960.[19]

In the late 60s I went with my mom to visit her friend, Toby, who was in the hospital recovering from breast cancer surgery. My mom happened to mention during the visit that she, too, had noticed a lump on her breast for quite a while. Toby asked if she'd had it checked and Mother replied that she had not. Toby said, "Tess, you need to go to the doctor right away."

Within a couple of days my mom followed Toby's advice and found out that she had breast cancer. She had surgery, and when I visited her in the hospital afterwards I was shocked at the size and appearance of her post-operative wounds. True to her nature, she claimed that it wasn't so bad. The cancer had progressed quickly by the time it was detected, and my mother passed away in 1970.

My father had a difficult time without her so he came to live with our family in our home in Lowell. After living without children for so many years, I think that he found that our home life was too chaotic. About this same time, an optometrist moved out of the building in which I had my offices, so we set up an apartment for my dad in that vacant office.

After my dad moved, a speaker at the Lions Club from Alcoholics Anonymous talked about the dangers of isolation. I spoke to him afterwards, and he convinced me of something that I should have realized myself: although Dad had everything he needed in that apartment and did not complain, he was not around other people, almost hibernating, which was not healthy. Dad needed his independence and peace, but also to be around other people. We found an apartment for him at Schneider Manor in Lowell where he could mingle with other seniors.

One night our son Jim had a ball game by the fair grounds, and we took my dad to watch it. He insisted on walking home afterwards. The next morning I went to his apartment and found that he had died in his sleep -- a beautiful way to go. I honestly think that he died of a broken heart; after my mom died, he did not have much of a will to live.

We sold my parents' house on Willard for $5000 after they died. There were forty houses for sale within a square mile around their neighborhood. While in the previous generation all of the houses had belonged to middle class while families, these neighborhoods were now becoming more diversified.

At the same time, "white flight" was occurring as many Caucasians left for the outskirts of Grand Rapids after the 1967 civil rights riots in Detroit, Michigan. Living in Lowell, we were rather isolated from the civil rights struggles. Now I read about how prevalent the KKK was, but again, I never heard any mention of it during the time that it was active. Of course, so much of the worst of the struggles and protests were in the southern states, and much of the fanaticism occurred in the rural areas.

Grand Rapids had undergone many changes during the time that I lived there, but it is still a conservative city comprised mostly of people with Dutch and other European ancestry. At one time Grand Rapids was the "Furniture Capital of the World" but many of the companies moved south. Grand Rapids, like Lowell, is a wonderful place to raise a family.

The kids surprised us in 1978 with this picture. I think they must have snuck Ed out the window right out from under Carol's nose! Back row: Mary, Karen, Jim, Jane and Kathy. Front row: Don, Ruth, Patty, Peggy and Ed.

Carol had taken piano lessons for eight years, and she would play beautiful classical pieces by Chopin and Beethoven. When she played Gershwin's *Rhapsody in Blue* it was just like being at Carnegie Hall. She inherited her parents' baby grand piano, and we insisted that each of the kids take piano for a year, but not one of them went further. Ed played the trombone for a couple years. The baby grand is still in the family at our daughter Ruth's home.

Because I'd never learned to swim, I felt it was important for our children to be comfortable in the water. Carol loved the water, and each of our kids was on Lowell's swim team. It was a big part of the summer.

Carol and I felt fortunate that we never really had many behavior problems with the kids. We hardly ever had to use physical force. Usually, when they misbehaved, they were denied certain privileges, and this seemed to teach them to behave better at times!

With such a big family, everyone had their share of work around the house. Maybe the work distribution didn't seem fair to all of them at the time, and we probably did give in more as the family grew. Carol and I may have been more strict with the first kids, and perhaps as we had more children we became more liberal. We probably let the younger ones skip their spinach every once in a while, but we still held on to the same core values.

With ten kids, we didn't have a lot of extra money. Carol and I felt it was important to provide some nice vacations, but even that was more challenging with so many little bodies. For three summers we rented a cottage on Silver Lake in Rockford, where my parents used to take our family when I was a boy, so it was somewhat nostalgic.

We rented a motor home and took the four oldest children to Yellowstone one year, and we took the six younger kids out West ten years later. Our family would also travel to Wisconsin, usually on holidays, to visit Carol's parents.

In the summer of 1964 we took the four oldest kids to the New York World's Fair. My greatest memory of that trip was when we saw the Pieta, a statue made by Michelangelo of the Virgin Mary holding Christ. This statue was normally kept in the Vatican In Rome, but was loaned to New York for this special occasion. Three duplicates of this Pieta were eventually made, and one is in front of St. Mary's Church in Spring Lake, Michigan.

The 1964/1965 New York World's Fair was the third major world's fair to be held in New York City. The fair's theme was "Peace Through Understanding", dedicated to "Man's Achievement on a Shrinking Globe in an Expanding Universe." The theme was symbolized by a 12-story high, stainless-steel model of the earth called the Unisphere.

UNISPHERE
United States Steel

NEW YORK WORLD'S FAIR 1964-1965

The fair is best remembered as a showcase of mid-20th century American culture and technology. The nascent Space Age was well-represented. Baby Boomers visited the optimistic fair as children before the turbulent years of the Vietnam War and increasing struggles for civil rights.

In many ways the fair symbolized a grand consumer show covering many products produced in America for transportation, living, and consumer electronics. Corporations demonstrated the use of mainframe computers, terminals with keyboards and CRT displays, decades before the Internet and home computers were at everyone's disposal.[20]

Canada's first World's Fair, Expo 67, was held in Montreal, Quebec, and had an international theme. Exhibits from all over the world were held in different pavilions, and you could get your "passport" stamped as you visited different countries' exhibits. Something ironic happened in the Russian exhibit. I had laid my camera down for some reason and left it behind when we exited the pavilion. When I finally realized what I had done I went back to see if someone had turned it in. I admit (and am embarrassed to say this) that I had a bit of a sense of mistrust because of our country's checkered history with Russia, so I was a little doubtful and assumed I'd never see that camera again. The lines to get in the Russian pavilion were extremely long, so I went to the side door. The people in charge of security said that someone had just turned my camera in, so I was pleasantly surprised!

About seven of my buddies and I had great fun building a 40' by 30' cabin on a 100-acre plot of land in Ferry, Michigan. Some of the guys were knowledgeable in various aspects of the building trade, so it was not just a little shanty. It had three bedrooms, a big living room, a kitchen and a bathroom with indoor plumbing! Tongue in cheek, we named it the OCHC, which stands for Oceana County Health Club. Probably because of the name, to this day I still receive so many magazines and catalogues that are targeted toward legitimate health clubs.

We set up an annual rotating schedule so that all of our families could use the cabin at different times of the year. Most of the guys used it as a hunting cabin, but I think that I was the only guy who didn't own a gun. Our family did go fishing occasionally in nearby Burt Lake. We took the family up for a couple of Christmases and became snowed in one year.

Over the years, we went to many amusement parks: Disneyworld in Florida and Cedar Point in Sandusky, Ohio. I was able to pass on my love of skiing to the kids, and many of my grandchildren enjoy it to this day. Our family went on many local ski trips to Cannonsburg, and often we would pack up and spend a few days in Boyne.

My friend Foster Bishop introduced me to skiing out West on a trip to Lake Tahoe in 1976. After a few years, I began to take some of the kids to some of these more challenging slopes as well.

Ready for a trip to Cannonsburg: Bob, Carol, Peggy, Jane, Jim (whose skis are hiding Jane's face), Karen, Mary and Kathy.

As the kids will tell you, my video camera was always at my side, and this type of venue was no exception. One day, I had taken some beautiful footage, but was ready to come down the mountain, so I zipped the camera in the front of my coat. As I was skiing down the mountain, I lost my balance and fell facedown in the snow. About 4:00 a.m. I woke up with chest pains, which scared the daylights out of my kids. The ER doctor gave us the good news that it was not a heart attack, but rather bruising around the rib muscles from landing on the camera!

Patty, Don, Ruth and Ed on that fateful trip out West.

I believe that all of these vacations enriched our lives in many ways, and it was enjoyable to have that extra family time. Even now, the kids retell many stories from our vacations.

Since my office was so close to our home, I rode my bike to work, even in the winter sometimes. I looked forward to coming home at noon every day to have lunch with my family, and was grateful that I didn't have to eat lunch at a local restaurant. Carol was a good cook, and since she learned from her mother, some of her dishes reflected that German influence.

One of our traditions was cooking hotdogs on the grill almost every Sunday night. I guess I have a hard time nowadays when I hear kids say they don't like this or that, or when they leave food on their plates. Our kids ate what they were given, and did not leave the table until they were finished. With ten kids, Carol had to be very creative at mealtimes, and she was very good at managing the home.

When Ed was about seven, Karen had moved out and she brought her dog to our house when she came for a visit. Ed took the dog for a walk around the neighborhood. Our neighbor, who happened to be outside, said, "Ed, that's a nice dog you have there."

Ed replied, "No, it's my sister's dog. We can't have a dog until our dad is dead." The neighbor called our house and repeated the story.

As I told the neighbor, Ed must have taken it literally when I told the kids, "Our family will get a dog over my dead body!"

Pope Paul VI promulgated the Novus Ordo Mass in 1969, which meant that Catholic churches could choose to say the Mass in a language other than Latin. Many parishes incorporated these changes, including our local church. Carol started attending a Roman Catholic Traditional Latin Mass in 1975, and by 1980 I began attending with her. We drove to a service in Kalamazoo where Father Carley would come up from Ohio to say the Mass in Latin. Over the centuries, having a service in Latin has helped unify Catholics from different countries and backgrounds; no matter where your location, you can go to a Traditional Latin Mass and know that the exact words are being spoken across the world in other traditional churches.

Beginning in 1990 the Society of St. Pius V served us from Detroit in a chapel in Grand Rapids. Later we purchased a church, also in Grand Rapids, and eventually a church was purchased in Allendale.

All of the kids except Don and Ed worked in my office for half the day during their senior year in high school. I feel that I got to know each of them better during that experience. They learned good work habits, and that dentistry can be hard work at times. They also were able to save enough money to pay for a couple of years of college. All of the kids went to college except for Patty, who was in the service for three years.

Carol and I enjoyed so many aspects of parenthood: watching the kids grow and develop as individuals, and encouraging them in their talents and interests. The home movies that we took during holidays and at reunions are so fun to watch, and I am working on converting them all to a more user-friendly format: DVD!

Watching the kids settle down and start their own families was also a source of pride and joy. As the kids grew up and started to move out of the house, it was always a challenge to rearrange the sleeping quarters. Sometimes the kids would stake a claim on the blue room or the basement room, etc. Life had always happened at a hectic pace, and it seemed strange when all of those extra rooms were not occupied anymore.

As people often say, one of the hardest things that a person can go through in life is losing a child. When our daughter Mary was killed in a car accident on August 11, 1979, our grief was overwhelming. Nothing can prepare you for something like that.

The last family picture that we took before we lost Mary, taken at Fallasburg Park: Back row: Peggy, Karen, Jane and Jim. Front row: Don, Patty, Kathy, Mary, Ruth and Ed.

The day before, on August 10, Carol and I were driving home from our cabin. It was a warm day, so Carol suggested that we go to Grand

Haven. We parked by the beach, and we were surprised when Mary and a couple of her girlfriends parked next to us. We spent some time together, and it was a lucky break that we saw her that evening. She lived in Grand Rapids at that time, and it was a common occurrence for her to visit the beach in Grand Haven with her friends in the evening to enjoy the sunset.

The next evening Carol and I went to the show, and when we got home the police were waiting in our driveway to notify us that Mary had been killed in a car accident on the way to Grand Haven.

I remember, at the funeral home, how people were so genuine in their sincerity in sharing our grief. We were surrounded by many loving and caring friends. Such a thing is so devastating that people don't know what words can really give comfort. Some people said to us that we were lucky that we had so many more children. Even though we felt so fortunate to be blessed with so many children, it does not soften the blow when one of them is gone. That's why, when I go to the funeral home after someone has lost a loved one I say very simply, "You are in my prayers," and I leave it at that.

It was only through the power of prayer and our faith that we were able to cope and get through that difficult time. Our faith has helped us through other trials as well, and I believe that because Carol and I had that common bond, we were able to avoid many troubles and problems.

We did not have a difficult time with the empty nest, probably because so many of the kids live so close and visit so often, it hardly seemed that they were gone!

After all of the kids moved out, Carol and I would join several other couples to go skiing up north. The tenth year of this, I was packing up the car in preparation to go to Boyne and she said, "Don't pack my skis." I asked what she meant, and she said, "The girls and I are going to cross country skiing. I never did like downhill."

I was flabbergasted and asked her why she had never told me. She said that she just wanted to be with the kids and me, and since we were having so much fun, she enjoyed herself, too. As I look back, the hills I took her on must have been a bit much for her, but she never complained. I have often wondered if there was anything else that she didn't care for but did not vocalize. Carol was so selfless. I don't think that she saw it as a sacrifice, either; she just accepted it as her role. I was a lucky guy to have her as my wife!

Historical Events and Signs of the Times

"There are no constraints on the human mind, no walls around the human spirit, no barriers to our progress except those we ourselves erect."
- Ronald Reagan (a.k.a. "Uncle Ronnie")

It is still hard for me to believe that man was able to land on the moon. We watched the Apollo 11 mission on television in July of 1969, and even as I was watching, I was so convinced that it was not possible until I saw with my own eyes when Neil Armstrong planted the flag on the moon's surface.

John F. Kennedy was shot in Dallas, Texas, on November 22, 1963, on Janie's tenth birthday. Two days later, I remember watching on television when the suspect, Lee Harvey Oswald, was shot by Jack Ruby while the cameras were rolling live.

When the United States became involved in the Korean War (1950s) and Vietnam War (1960s) it was so hard for me to believe that the peace that so many had worked to attain in World War II did not last very long. Knowing the huge toll that World War II had on so many individuals, in so many different ways, we were hoping that the United States wouldn't be involved in another armed conflict so soon.

The soldiers who went to Korea and Vietnam (or Iraq or Afghanistan recently) were not always welcomed back with open arms. Many people are against U.S. involvement in conflicts in which we are not in direct danger, so those veterans were not shown the same respect and honor and may not have felt affirmed in their service. Today, when vets come back home it's harder for them to get back in the mainstream because job opportunities are so limited. We, as World War II vets, did not experience such hardships.

It became necessary to keep up with technology while I was practicing. Calculators made billing and bookkeeping much easier in the 1960s. Computers became commonplace in offices in the 1980s, and although I put this technology off for quite a while, I realized eventually that it did make things easier. My accountant admitted to me that after he went to a computerized system, he also kept track of the books manually for about three years until he was convinced that the computers were trustworthy! It is mind-boggling that kids use computers at such a young age school, and it is hard to imagine what education will look like in another generation.

In the 1960s, the first advertisements for calculators were obviously targeted toward men, as it was assumed that men would be making the purchasing decisions for most office equipment. The first models were bulky and cumbersome. Every year the new models were more sleek and efficient.

Car phones became popular at about the same time. The first ones were a lot bigger and clumsier than the cell phones of today, and they did not do half as much! With all new technology, the earliest models were very expensive, and then the prices went down a bit.

In the area of medicine, penicillin was an incredible advancement. A lot of lives were saved during World War II, and of course since then, with the administration of these "wonder drugs." Even so, many soldiers died during the service due to disease and illnesses that they picked up overseas. One example is my friend, Bill Brunner, who died of a native strain of influenza while stationed in the Philippine Islands.

In 1929 Alexander Fleming, a doctor and researcher at St. Mary's Hospital in London, England, published a paper on a chemical he called "penicillin", which he had isolated from a mold, Penicillium notatum. Penicillin, Fleming wrote, had prevented the growth of a neighboring colony of germs in the same petri dish. Fleming was never able to purify his samples of penicillin, but he became the first person to publish the news of its germ-killing power. Howard Florey, Ernst Chain and Norman Heatley expanded on Fleming's work in 1938, at Oxford University. They and their staff developed methods for growing, extracting and purifying enough penicillin to prove its value as a drug.

World War II had begun by the time their research was showing results. The main research and production was moved to the United States in 1941, to protect it from the bombs pounding England. Work began on how to grow the mold efficiently to make penicillin in the large quantities that would be needed for thousands of soldiers. As the destruction of the war grew, so did interest in penicillin in laboratories, universities and drug companies on both sides of the Atlantic. The scientists knew they were in a race against death, because an infection was as likely to kill a wounded soldier as the wound itself. Today, in the United States, deaths by infectious bacterial diseases are only one-twentieth of what they were in 1900, before any antibiotic chemicals had been discovered. We would be shocked to hear of someone dying from an infection that started in a scratch, but before antibiotics like penicillin, it was common for people to die from such infections.[21]

(I upgraded my hot tub over the years as well, much to the enjoyment of my grandchildren!)

Giving Back

"To know even one life has breathed easier because you have lived. This is to have succeeded." - Ralph Waldo Emerson

I know that I have been blessed in my life with many lucky breaks. Maybe that's why I have always been motivated to give back to society. Since I would never have been able to afford dental school if it were not for the G.I. Bill, continuing to serve my country in other ways has been a big part of my life.

When I served on the Church board at St. Mary's and on Parish Council, the issues could at times be emotionally charged. People would object to decisions and sometimes their criticism would get personal. Carol would ask me how it was possible for me to associate with people who said nasty things and told me I was doing a lousy job. The way I explained it to Carol, the critics did not know all of the facts. They were upset, and that's the way they expressed it, so I did not take it personally. As a board, we were aware of all of the facts and carefully weighed all the options, so I was always comfortable with the decisions we made.

I was on the Lowell School Board of Education for twelve years, serving as president for seven of those years. Sometimes the criticism that we faced for some of our decisions became even more pointed. People would lambaste us, and some of them were not even in the district. Again, they were only considering their side, and could not see the whole picture. I received some nasty letters from people who did not know all the facts. Sometimes the criticism would even be featured in the newspaper. Again, that did not bother me since I always felt that the Board had thoroughly researched and discussed the issues and made fair decisions.

I have always felt that it is important to be involved in civic affairs. It was an honor to receive the 1993 Distinguished Service Award from the West Michigan Dental Society.

The West Michigan Dental Society
presents its
1993 DISTINGUISHED
SERVICE AWARD
to

ROBERT E. REAGAN, D.D.S.

Thursday, February 11, 1993

ROBERT E. REAGAN, D.D.S

"The Affable Irishman"

In America today, people are having great difficulty assessing what constitutes a family, and what impact family values have on the ills of America.

The 1993 recipient of the West Michigan District Dental Society Distinguished Service Award is Robert Emmett Reagan, D.D.S. An overview of his private, family, civic, and professional life might serve as a guide of how to apply family values so that America would be enriched throughout all its land if his example were followed.

Bob was the oldest of six children, born to an Irish heritage family, whose home life was one of structured discipline. The children were loved and nurtured, but order was necessary in their lifestyle. Since grade school Bob held jobs working as a Press Carrier, Goebel & Brown Sport Shop clerk, college janitor, post office worker, factory worker, along with painting jobs. A life of industry became his style. He was one of those people who did not stand still - never walked when he could run to accomplish things. The level of responsibility that his parents and bosses gave him are what make him today a man of purpose. He's a man who developed character and integrity at a young age and his commitment in life fully demonstrates how much he was helped by those early beginnings.

Bob's high school days were filled with sports (baseball, basketball, football) and by his admission, he was not a "standout", but a team player, filling in when needed. When you discuss Bob with his colleagues they say the same thing. He always responds when needed, so we can dispute his not being a high school "standout."

When his service years ended he was encouraged to use his G.I. Bill to become a dentist, and graduated from Marquette University School of Dentistry in 1953. A close review of his biographical profile shows he started a lifetime of people-oriented commitment about the time he began his dental career, and has carried through to the present. All his family training, schooling, and sideline occupations enhanced what we know today as Bob Reagan, the man with the infectious grin. His achievements are overshadowed by his concern for his family, and one might ask - how did this all happen? Well, his early training prepared him, but it's his life mate, Carol, who kept all the glue of family life together. A man does not raise ten children and be an active leader without a helper who keeps the home fires glowing as did Carol. You can just imaging the chaos in a home of ten children with an active, community-oriented father, if a strong wife and mother were not present. Two of his daughters summed up what others shared also, that they "loved Dad for his love through good and bad times, but mostly for his love, respect, and loyalty to Mom. He was the leader—she was the heart."

Time and life's experiences have helped Bob in a unique way as expressed by a fellow dentist: "He has found real happiness by balancing his time and energy among true values. His faith, his profession, recreation, friends and family are richer because of the love he has shown us."

Let's review what other colleagues say about our Award recipient: "A good family man — does more than he's asked; I appreciate his slow smile as he greets me; consistent and steady in habits; good 'ole' reliable; his genuine friendship and smile; his personality; he is truly a funny person—his humor cracks me up; friendly, positive and caring; what a golfer!; always offers a cheerful 'yes' when asked to help; dedicated family man; a truly civic-minded individual who always finds time to help." Naturally the list could go on with many accolades, but these give insight as to the man we honor today.

Bob's response to "what makes you tick?" is typical. He said, "In a small town you use your talents, and once involved, you keep getting more involved. I've rarely said no when asked to do something."

This unusual individual bikes to his office, loves Irish heritage, lunches at home at noon, and constantly seeks to help as he passes through life.

As you attempt to characterize our recipient you are repeatedly alerted to two factors that have tracked throughout his biographical profile: his love for God and church by using his faith to do good works, and his love of, and service to, his family. All his activities rotate around these drives of his life. All the morals that people attribute to church and family are embodied in his lifestyle. But, also, his is not just a willingness to serve by filling a seat; he is also a participant in all his endeavors, as his colleagues relate.

To totally capsulize a life of 60-plus years is not possible in a document of this size. When you see all the activities listed, plus a family of ten children, you have to be amazed at what one man has accomplished. One of his kids said, "Dad, we're glad you're ours." West Michigan District Dental Society can say, "Bob, we're glad you're ours, too. What a pleasure to honor you with our Silent Bell Award!"

"Service - Service - Service"

Born: February 16, 1926 in Grand Rapids, Michigan (one of six children)
Family: Wife Carol (nee: Callan), ten children (ages 19 to 34, 7 girls, 3 boys)
Education: • St. Francis Xavier (Grand Rapids) Grade School
  • 1944 graduate, Grand Rapids Catholic Central High School
  • 1946-48 - Grand Rapids Junior College
  • 1948-53 - Marquette University Dental School (D.D.S.)
Church: • 31 years - St. Mary's Parish
  - Parish Council, 12 years (1972 - President)
  - Men's Club, 31 years (Sec/Treas, 25 years)
  - catechism, 5 years for High School-aged students
  • presently - St. Margaret Mary of the Sacred Heart Church
  - served as usher, finances chair, development fund, Parish fund drives
  - on committee to establish a traditional Catholic Chapel
Military Service:
  • 1944-1946, U.S. Air Force
  - T/Sgt Rank, Tail gunner, South Pacific Service
Hobbies: Family, snow skiing, camping, biking, baseball as youth, tennis, cards (euchre & poker), all Michigan professional teams fan, and naturally golf, golf, golf, and more golf.
Civic Commitment:
  • Schools
  - 1962-1974, Member, Lowell Public Schools Board
  - 1963-67, Secretary
  - 1967-74, President
  - Millage Committees, New High School, Shop Area Development, etc.
  - 1962-76, Member, Michigan and National School Board Associations
  • Lowell Lions Club
  - Charter Member, 1954
  - 1955, President
  - 1954-60, Director
  - 1968-present, Editor, Club Bulletin
  - Committees (flags, program, public relations, membership greetings, sports, nominations, etc.)
  • Lowell Show Boat - 1959-60, Endman
  • Lowell Community United Way Fund - 35 years, Secretary/Treasurer

- Lowell Chamber of Commerce
  - 1953-present, member
  - 1956, President
  - 1991, received "Person of the Year" Award
  - Helped bring Atwood Brass Company to Lowell
- Lowell City Affairs
  - 1961-66, Planning Committee; helped write City Charter that still serves
  - 1966-73, Zoning Board and Appeals Board
- Lowell Order of Moose
  - 1972-present, member
- Clark Ellis Post, American Legion
  - 1953-present, member
- Lowell Savings and Loan Association
  - 1977-87, Board member
- Grand Rapids Serra Club (to guide boys to priesthood)
  - 1955-60, member
  - 1957, Essay Awards Chairman
  - 1958, Program Chairman

Professional Contributions:
- 1953-present, Private Dental practice
- 1953-present, Member, Kent County Dental Society
- 1953-present, Member, West Michigan Dental Society
  - 1965, President
  - 1963-64, Program Chairman
  - 1967-69, Editor, West Michigan Dental Bulletin (First Editor)
  - 1980-83, Legislative Committee (1980 Chairman)
  - 1983-89, Member, Peer Review Committee
- 1953-present, Member, Michigan Dental Association
  - 1960-62, State Insurance Program
- 1955, Helped institute Fluoridation Program in Lowell
- 1983-present, Member, West Michigan Dental Foundation Board of Trustees
  - 1983, Chaired first fund raising campaign
  - 1989-91, President
  - Committees (Campaign Fund Raising, Nominations, Annual Meeting)

Recognitions:
- 1984, Member, American College of Dentists
- 1991, Lowell City Chamber of Commerce "Person of the Year" Award

PREVIOUS RECIPIENTS OF THE SILENT BELL AWARD

I believe that we should share as much as we can with those less fortunate. I do believe that it is important to help our own first. In my practice, I often reduced fees for the patients that were having trouble making ends meet. Another organization in which I have been involved is the Adult Needs Program in Kent County. I've tried to support worthwhile charity programs, and I could probably do more, but sometimes it's hard to know which ones are truly worthwhile!

Closing Up Shop

"It is a rare and difficult attainment to grow old gracefully and happily." –
Arnold Palmer

After practicing 40½ years, I made the decision to retire at the age of sixty-eight in 1994. By this time, my son Jim had been practicing with me for eight years, so I think that may have made it easier for me to leave. It was a pleasure for all those years to watch Jim mature as a dentist and improve in his techniques, and it was also beneficial for both of us to bounce ideas and thoughts off of one another as colleagues. He kept the office in the family, and I was very proud to pass the baton to him.

After I retired I spent a lot of time in the basement, where I had everything I needed for my hobbies: my computer, workbench, scrapbooks, reunion material and church books. I think that my retirement was an adjustment for Carol as well, as she would often say to me, "Isn't it time for you to go down to the basement?" But we appreciated the extra time together. Our lifestyle did not change that much; we never lived high on the hog.

We joined the snowbird crowd and began going to Lakeland, Florida, for the winter months the year after I retired. There are 510 units in the park, and about 1/3 of the people are from Michigan, probably because the Detroit Tigers' training stadium is in Lakeland. Many of us enjoy the pre-season games, which begin in March. We joined a euchre club and played lots of golf as well.

After church on Sundays Carol and I would have breakfast at the nearby Fantasy of Flight Center, which features the world's greatest collection of restored airplanes from the beginning of the history of flight, including many WWII aircraft.

There would often be speakers who talked about their WWII experiences, including representatives from the Red Tail Squadron, a crew of African American pilots in the Tuskegee training program who faced segregation but still did their part.

It was a tradition to have a St. Patrick's Day party at our home for years, and about 100 people would celebrate with us. Now Peggy and Jim each have a party, but they have them on different days so our family can go to both parties.

To celebrate our 25th wedding anniversary, Carol and I took a trip to Hawaii. Over the years we had the privilege of attending a couple of dental conventions in Hawaii as well. *The U.S.S. Arizona* Memorial in Honolulu opened in 1980; visiting the Pearl Harbor Memorial was meaningful and brought back memories.

The 6th Bomb Group Association began having reunions in 1987, and I've had the opportunity to attend many of them. While there were about 2900 guys in our group during WWII, about 250 attended the first reunion, and the numbers keep dwindling. They are held all over the country; in the fall of 2012 I hope to attend a reunion in Charleston, South Carolina. When we get together we relive the days in training and the time on Tinian, and as often happens, the stories keep getting better!

Me, Paul Tibbetts (pilot of the Enola Gay) and Virgil Morgan at the 6th Bomb Association reunion in 2000.

I dust off my uniform once a year when I march in the Memorial Day Parade in Lowell. Only about fifteen WWII veterans currently march. Not many vets from the Korean and Vietnam Wars march, probably because of the mixed feelings about U.S. involvement in those wars.

Kathy and I, Memorial Day, 2007.

All of these years since WWII, the Enola Gay was sitting outside, left to the elements, and there was talk that it was going to be restored and placed in the Smithsonian Museum in Washington, D.C. But the proposed accompanying exhibit implied that the United States was the aggressor in World War II. Many people felt that the Director and the committee were attempting to rewrite history and because of an uproar from veterans, the exhibit was pulled and the Director and some of the committee members lost their jobs.

Martin Harwit, director of the Smithsonian's National Air and Space Museum, has resigned because of the controversy over a recent proposed exhibit for the Enola Gay, the B-29 that delivered the first atomic weapon. Responding to pressure from veterans groups, 81 Congressmen demanded the exhibit be rejected. Harwit described the Enola Gay exhibition incident as "the most violent dispute ever witnessed by a museum."

The Enola Gay lay rotting in a field at Andrews Air Force Base, Washington, D.C., becoming a victim of the weather, corrosive bird droppings and even vandals looking for souvenirs. Then it was moved to a hangar at Suitland, Maryland. Veterans urged the museum to restore the plane, so in the mid 1980s the museum began restoring the plane for exhibition. Harwit says the museum took great care to collect history surrounding the Enola Gay to create an informative exhibit. Months prior to the exhibition, veterans groups lobbied Congress to withdraw funding because they felt the museum was portraying the military bombing of Hiroshima in a light unflattering to Americans. In January 1995 the Smithsonian's new secretary, I. Michael Heyman, bowed to that pressure.

In explaining to Congress why the exhibition was canceled, Heyman wrote: "We made a basic error in attempting to couple an historical treatment of the use of atomic bombs with the 50th anniversary commemoration of the end of the war..[Veterans and their families] were not looking for analysis, and frankly, we did not give enough thought to the intense feelings such an analysis would evoke." It was decided the plane would be exhibited alone, devoid of historical context, which pleased the veterans and Congress. A few months later, Harwit resigned.[22]

Carol and I were able to take some very nice trips. We went to Ireland together twice, and another time I went with some golf buddies. The deal I made with Carol was that, for every cathedral we visited, we would also visit an Irish pub! One of the biggest thrills of my life was when Carol and I marched in the 1991 St. Patrick's Day Parade in Dublin, Ireland.

Thousands of people marched in the parade, and we all wore our festive attire. There was such excitement in the air, and the spectators were very enthusiastic, to say the least! We booked the trip through DeVries Travel Agency (ironically, Hollanders!); about forty of us hit many hot spots throughout our beloved Eire. I received a plaque engraved with a picture of St. Patrick's Cathedral from a travel agency representative. He often asked our opinions of the different locations on our trip, and I really buttered everything up, so I think that earned me some points.

Ballybunion Golf Club, County Kerry, Ireland, 1994.
Back row: O'Brien, Reagan, Rector, Skiba, Yahne; Front Row: Johnson, Neff

The Elderhostel program allowed us to learn many things, and helped us to meet some fascinating people. These programs were hosted by various universities across the United States, and would begin on Monday and conclude on Friday or Saturday. The ones that Carol and I attended were primarily in the south and the west. We'd sign up for three sessions in Arizona, Texas or Florida, and two in Georgia over a six-week period.

Between each weekly session we would take a week to travel around the area and do some sightseeing. During each weekly session, the university would feature three different subjects. There were history selections (for example, Kennedy's assassination or the Civil War), music (usually the #1 choice), nature studies (canyons, cacti, owls etc.), art, and even golf! The speakers were always tremendous and very knowledgeable.

Part of the Elderhostel fee went toward room and board, and we would stay on campus. These trips kept our minds active and we always learned so much. I had constant reminders that Carol was smarter than I was!

The U.S.S. Lexington, known as "The Blue Ghost," is one of 24 Essex-class aircraft carriers built during WWII. The ship is now in Corpus Christie, Texas.

Elderhostel was founded by Marty Knowlton, a world-traveling, free-spirited social activist and former educator, and David Bianco, a highly organized university administrator. Knowlton had recently returned from a four-year walking tour of Europe, carrying only a backpack of bare essentials and staying in youth hostels. Knowlton was also impressed with institutions in Scandinavia, called folk schools. There, he saw older adults handing down age-old traditions - folk art, music, lore and dance - to younger generations. Seeing Europeans in their 60s, 70s and 80s playing an active and positive role in their communities made Knowlton wonder why their American counterparts didn't have a similar opportunity to remain active after retirement.

Back in the U.S., Knowlton shared stories of his travels with Bianco. Why should older Americans be expected to disappear quietly into a mundane retirement? Bianco said, in a burst of enthusiasm, "This campus ought not to be having a youth hostel, it ought to be having an elder hostel." The name was born, and a learning program was conceived that combined stimulating, not-for-credit classes on a wide variety of subjects with comfortable, inexpensive lodgings.

In the summer of 1975, five colleges and universities in New Hampshire offered the first Elderhostel programs to 220 "pioneer" participants. In 1980, based almost entirely on word-of-mouth promotion, more than 20,000 participated in programs in all 50 states and most Canadian provinces.

Riding this growing wave of enthusiasm, Elderhostel offered its first international programs in 1981 in Mexico, Great Britain, and Scandinavia. Combining education with travel to foster experiential learning, they afforded participants the opportunity to discover the people, culture, environment, and history of the countries visited through lectures, course-

related field trips, cultural excursions, and extracurricular activities.

February 1994: Page, Arizona, Rainbow Bridge National Monument.

Today the programs continue to be offered, but they have been renamed as the Road Scholar programs. At the heart of today's organization are the participants, who are lifelong learners engaged in programs that foster camaraderie and a sense of community. [23]

    I think that Carol and I had the same general outlook on life, which made our relationship easier. It also made raising the kids easier because we saw eye to eye. Carol and I always lived pretty simply, and never cared too much about "stuff." We had a wonderful marriage, and our love grew stronger every year. The biggest contributing factor was our deep religious faith. We both had complete trust in one another; I was faithful to her, and she was faithful to me. We also had the same goals and values, and our traits complemented one another.

Since Carol's field was nursing, she was familiar with various courses of treatment. Through reading medical journals, she kept abreast of current trends and treatments in nursing. Her tremendous memory constantly impressed me; no matter what I brought up in our conversations, she remembered examples from her training in the hospital.

Our extended family enjoyed many excursions at the OCHC cabin.

Carol kept exceptionally accurate medical histories of all the children. I just found them recently and passed them along to the kids; the detail is unbelievable. Once again, it shows that she had a phenomenal memory, far greater than mine.

When our children became parents themselves, they would call Carol when their kids were sick. They'd describe the symptoms to Carol, and she'd tell them what she thought it was. Sure enough, they'd take the kids to the doctor, who would confirm Carol's diagnosis. So even though Carol did not receive a paycheck, she did practice nursing and was a great resource for her children and grandchildren.

Carol was diagnosed with non-Hodgkins lymphoma in 1995. For eleven years she received treatment that was pretty routine, and she handled it beautifully. She felt so good, and it did not slow her down; we continued to travel and enjoy retirement. In 2006 things took a turn for the worse. We were able to get an apartment in Schneider Manor. In May 2007 we returned to our home on King Street, which we had not sold.

At 4:00 p.m. on October 11, one of our children showed up without being called. Then another came, and then another. When the whole family had gathered, we called the priest. As he was giving Carol the Final Rites at 7:00 p.m. she closed her eyes for the last time.

I think that women can handle the death of their partner far better than men. I believe that many widowed men have died of a broken heart, or have lost their will to live after their life's partner passes away. When I lost Carol there was an emptiness in my heart that is impossible to explain.

My kids decided that a trip would be good for me, so In 2008 I went to Ireland with five of them: Jane, Karen, Kathy, Jim and Peggy. We visited beautiful cathedrals and many traditional Irish pubs.

2008, at an Irish pub: Jim, me, Peggy, Jane and Karen.

The common theme of our trip was that we got lost every day. The cars were tiny, so we rented two cars for the six of us. After about the third or forth time we got lost it became predictable but also a little ridiculous, so we'd pull off to the side and just laugh like fools.

One day were drove past a field and we stopped the cars because some of the kids noticed a campground with lots of big tents. They thought they'd strike up a conversation with the campers, but when we got closer we realized that the "tents" were mounds of turf covered with canvas. The Irish use the turf, or peat, to heat their homes. The kids had a local artist make a painting based on a photograph that we took. The painting is titled "Irish Campers" and it hangs in a prominent place, along with a block of turf, in my apartment.

In October of 2010 I had successful gall bladder surgery. The doctors took many x-rays at that time, and nothing else was revealed. The next spring, in April of 2011, I had some problems with my wrist, and I had limited use in a couple of my fingers. The doctor decided to take a chest x-ray before I had my surgery. I'd had a persistent cough, but that did not seem alarming, since so many of my friends in Florida also suffered from colds at that time.

The Reagan family, 2001: our 50th wedding celebration!

The x-rays that the doctor took revealed a mass in my chest. Further testing revealed that I had neuroendocrine cancer and I soon began chemotherapy treatment. In December 2011 x-rays revealed that tumors in my prostate and lungs were gone, but I still had cancer in my abdomen.

For a while I was on oral chemo, but am currently going to the Lemmen Holt Pavilion for intravenous treatment every three weeks. The nurses are so kind, considerate and thoughtful. My nurse, Tammy, knew Carol, and every time I go, other nurses will stop and talk and encourage me. I feel pretty doggone lucky, as my illness has not slowed me down too much. The treatments are an inconvenience and I've lost my hair, but it could be so much worse!

In October 2011 my daughter Karen and I went to France with a group of forty people, including priests and seminarians. This was the journey of a lifetime for me. I had never dreamed I would make such a trip, especially in light of the fact that I was in the middle of chemotherapy treatments.

Our group landed in Paris, and over the next few days we visited many shrines and cathedrals throughout France. Such visits were both humbling and breathtaking; to spend time in these buildings of astounding craftsmanship puts you in a place of deep reverence and awe when you consider the history of the people who made so many contributions and sacrifices. This was a foreshadowing of what we would experience in Lourdes. We spent four days in Lourdes, a market town in the foothills of the Pyrenees Mountains. This town is especially significant because it was here that Our Lady appeared to Bernadette Soubirous, a

The Golden Crown graces the top of the Rosary Basilica in Lourdes, France.

little shepherd girl, in 1858 when she went to the grotto for some water. A beautiful shrine at the grotto commemorates Our Lady's appearances to Bernadette.

Thousands of people make a pilgrimage to this shrine every day, and although I knew it would be meaningful, I was overcome with wonder when I visited the shrine at the grotto. Although there were so many other visitors, I would say that there was a consistent feeling of deep devotion and reverence amongst the entire crowd, as we realized we were in a miraculous place. That trip had such an impact on both of us.

Even this past winter I was able to go to Florida. Here in Lowell, I enjoy visiting with the other residents at Schneider Manor. My children take such good care of me, taking me to treatments and having me over

for dinner frequently. I allow myself one game of solitaire on the computer every day, and I still play golf every Monday! My days are pleasant and peaceful, and I am surrounded by wonderful people!

Looking Back on My Life

"God, grant me the serenity to accept the things I cannot change, the courage to change the things I can, and the wisdom to know the difference." – Reinhold Niebuhr

I've had a lot of time to think about my life lately. Although I do not have any major regrets:

I wish that I'd have played less golf. It was such an escape for me when I was a dentist, and it was a way for me to blow off steam at the end of a long day, but I now realize that at the same time, it put more of a burden on Carol. I wish I had thought more about her and spent more time with our children. When you make decisions you can't foresee all of the consequences, and unfortunately, all of us learn lessons the hard way because either we are too young or too stubborn.

I wish that I'd have said "No" more often when it comes to civic duties, although I still feel that it is very important to give back. I spent many hours in meetings that I could have spent with my family. I got so involved in so many organizations, and although I enjoyed it all, I could have been a better dad and husband if I had been more protective of my free time.

Citizen of the Year ceremony at Deer Run.

I wish that I had learned to spell better. It's funny what you remember, but always being the first one down in the spelling bee (in the good company of my buddy Tom!) is very vivid in my mind. Fortunately, when you misspell "penicillin," nobody catches it, and medical professionals are notorious for writing messy prescriptions, so it did not impact my professional life too much. Carol saved me from grammatical blunders because she edited everything I wrote!

I wish I had pushed myself harder to learn how to swim.

I wish I'd told Carol that I loved her more often. Although I said it every day, I should have said it all the time.

My 65th Birthday.

The Way I See It

"If you want others to be happy, practice compassion. If you want to be happy, practice compassion." - Dalai Lama

All of the advancements in the world, I believe, are a double-edged sword. Along with the progress of the digital age comes the availability of too much information, which can be dangerous for young people and adults as well. It seems that as time goes on it will be increasingly difficult to lead a virtuous lifestyle unless the Church returns to the basic beliefs and people care for one another as they should. My biggest fear concerns the government being involved in controlling our lives: what we see, hear, believe, and know. We need strong, moral world leaders. Over the years, it has been surprising to observe how increasingly mobile society has become. People are on the road at all times of the year, and life exists at a much faster pace, but sometimes it would benefit all of us to just slow down a bit.

Society has also become so much more prosperous, as evidenced by bigger homes, fancy cars and more and more impressive golf courses! It concerns me that the Church has also become much more liberal. Ideally, there will be a shift of people returning to a deeper faith in God, with less emphasis on material things. Although earthly pleasures and possessions will not help in getting a person to heaven, that is what seems to be the focus for so many people today.

Memorial Day 2011.

Something I desire for my children and grandchildren, and for society in general, is that people learn to be content with what they have. It seems that nowadays people are always wanting more, and getting it. From my parents' generation I learned to save what I earned and to pay cash. Since people starting using plastic (credit cards) it has become hard for some to put a limit on spending.

When I watch the news I wonder why there is so much senseless crime in the world; so much of it is rooted in greed and jealousy. The wars and conflicts seem so senseless.

Greed is also evident in the legal system; it seems that people are increasingly eager to sue and to gain financially whenever they are wronged. I believe that people are responsible for their own actions, and should admit when they are wrong instead of using the court system to resolve disputes.

The best advice that I have for my children is that honesty is the best policy. Be straightforward when dealing with people. Practice what you preach. I'm not great at giving advice; I hope that I can accomplish more by setting an example.

Mothers Day 2010 in front of the Lowell Showboat: Peggy, Karen, me, Jane, Patty, Kathy and Ruth.

My overall guide for living has always been the Golden Rule: Do unto others as you would have them do to you. Also, try to see something good in everyone, and don't be envious of those around you. It makes life so much easier and less complicated if you try to focus on the positives!

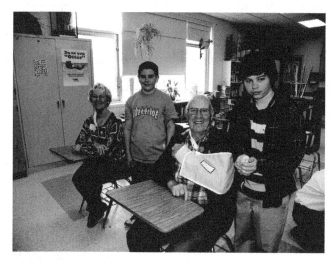

Grandfriends Day, Ada Christian School, May 2011: Aunt Jane, Vinnie, me and Frankie.

Although I have enjoyed traveling, I do not have a strong desire to go anywhere now. I suppose I'd love to play on the Augusta National Golf Club in Georgia where the Masters Tournament is held every year. I have been to Augusta four times, and there is such a mystique about that course, but it is very protected. I do wish that I could have taken my folks to Ireland, and I regret that I did not visit the town of Callan with Carol, since this was her ancestors' hometown. Some of my friends in Florida love to see the world; they talk about going on Caribbean cruises and African safaris, and I am happy for them but have no personal desire to go to exotic places. I have an inner contentment with my simple life.

Thanksgiving 2011, sharing a toast with Seven Daughters Wine. Back row: Ruth, Kathy, Peggy, Jane, Becky. Front row: Karen, me and Patty.

If I were to suddenly inherit a million dollars I would try to get a pool for the city of Lowell in the YMCA. Maybe a million dollars would only be enough money to dig the hole, but that could provide the momentum to finish the rest! I have been a member of the Lions Club since 1955 (I'm the only charter member left!), and years ago a woman gave $500,000 to the city for the purpose of building a pool. The pool that was built had problems for about twenty years, so it was filled in, and the residents have been without a pool since. Having the pool was such a tremendous advantage for our kids when they were growing up, and I wish that other children could have that same opportunity.

If I could meet anyone in the course of the world's history I would love to meet one of the saints, and St. Patrick would be at the top of the list. Also, Mother Theresa served God as I wished I could. I still love to read about the Civil War, so Abraham Lincoln would also be fascinating to meet. I have admired the determination of many athletes: Babe Ruth, Hank Greenberg, Billy Rogell, Micky Cochrane, and Charlie Gehringer (baseball); Tom Harmon (football); Ben Hogan, Arnold Palmer Jack Nicklaus (golf).

If I had not been a dentist, I think I would have been well-suited to politics. I believe I could do a better job than today's politicians are doing. I got a bit of a taste for what politicians go through when I served on the Lowell School Board. I realized that, although there would so many things that I would have liked to accomplish, we were limited in what we could do in reality. Politicians make all kinds of promises, but it seems that they are out of touch with reality. While it is beneficial that there are two parties, it is disappointing that politicians spend so much time and effort knocking down the other's programs. They talk about compromise but that, too, seems insincere.

If something wasn't going well in my civic duties or in my professional life, I always tried to stay calm and never got too excited. I always figured that somehow I'd come out of the situation better than I was before. There were plenty of dental failures that turned out well in the end! Maybe some people would interpret that approach to life as rather dull, but that's my nature, and I have always felt that it was better to remain as calm as possible. I do kind of enjoy it when I see how excited people can get at football games for a touchdown or on the golf course for an excellent shot, but on the flipside, throwing clubs and yelling at the refs never seems to accomplish anything. For me, prayer seems much more effective, and I have always tried to approach all of life's events and circumstances that way.

What's Most Important

"The power of prayer can overcome all of our problems. Sometimes it just seems to take longer than we wish!" - Robert Emmett Reagan

As I have gotten older I have realized more and more that family is so important! That may sound like a cliché, but it is so true. I was brought up in such a tremendously strong, faithful and supportive family. When I needed advice, I always felt comfortable going to my parents. I wish that I'd taken the time to learn about their childhoods, and even their parents' (my grandparents') life situations, to know what shaped them. Since I was very close to my aunts and uncles, I was also comfortable looking to them for guidance. I always looked forward to being with my cousins when we were growing up, and we all got along so well.

My extended family has remained close, and some of my siblings even became my dental patients, which must prove that they trusted me! My sister, Mary, was also diagnosed with breast cancer in 2000, and she passed away on November 23, 2002.

The Reagan clan, 2008: Tom, Mike, Pat (Butch), Patty and Bob.

We have had many family reunions, some in Lowell, and over the years we have shared in each other's joys and sorrows. It's so important for families to do things together, and that is something that I hope Carol and I instilled in our children.

I am so proud of each and every one of my children and would never want to compare them to one another. If they are happy in what they are doing, that is what is important. I am also proud that they all get along so well with each other. Of course there have been times when things got a little touchy, but none of them seem to hold a grudge, at least not for long. None of them has ever expressed to me that they are jealous of another sibling. I give Carol the credit for how well the kids turned out, as she did 80% of the parenting and I only did 20%. I know that I can't force my children to believe everything that I believe, but when we don't see eye to eye, there is still mutual respect.

My twenty-three grandkids all live in this area, for which I am very thankful, and they know each other pretty well. Carol and I used to enjoy having them stay overnight.

My oldest grandchild, Emily Myers Thuja, becomes a bride in 2010.

My grandchildren are all so unique, and it has been a joy to watch them grow and change. I had a special love for my grandparents and hope to foster the same relationship with my grandchildren.

Having close friends has also sustained me. I admire people who can see some good in every situation, and I consciously choose to surround myself with people who embody that trait. It is always more pleasant to be around people who enjoy life and look at the bright side instead of complain. Carol was brought up with that attitude, which was one of the reasons she was so enjoyable to be around. Kindness goes a long way in solving problems and getting along with one another. There is good in everyone. You have to look beyond people's flaws.

I've had some incredible opportunities with different groups of people. There have been so many people in my life who have given me encouragement and guidance. Although I was not the greatest student, I always felt so affirmed and trusting of the nuns and priests at school, starting with St. Francis. Tom Zoellner has continued to be a close friend since kindergarten. I loved being a part of various teams, even when I did not get a lot of playing time! I'll never underestimate the benefits of my time in the service. I met smart, brave, patriotic men who were happy to serve our country. There were many men in the Lowell area that I looked up to: Herb Elzinga, Ernie Foreman and King Doyle to name a few.

All my adult life I have been surrounded by wonderful people: as acollege student, in my practice, in organizations and on committees, and in recreational activities such as golf and euchre!

Bob Reagan and King Doyle, 2009.

Finally, I have learned that when you are experiencing problems, it is important to have faith. Prayer has been such a big part of my life from the time I was a child, and it has only become more important throughout the years. I say the rosary every night before I go to bed. Carol and I used to pray together every night; she told me that she prayed an hour every day. It was her nature to pray. I believe that the Irish heritage, which we had in common, was one of the reasons that our faith was so important to both of us. My daughter Karen still takes me to Traditional Latin Mass at St. Margaret Mary in Allendale, and when I'm in Florida I go sixty-two miles to attend Traditional Latin Mass in Tavares.

If I could ask God anything, I'd ask for His forgiveness. Like other believers, I try to follow the Ten Commandments and the six commandments of the Catholic Church. I believe that, when people die,

187

God will judge them as only a just judge can. They will either join Him in heaven or spend eternity in hell. We should pray for the dead, because it is possible for the souls who are in Purgatory to gain heaven.

Satan is constantly working on us to leave our faith, and temptations surround us. The evil in the world is all Satan's making, but sometimes we cooperate with him. I look back at my life, and even though there have been difficult times, I have never been swayed from or let go of my faith. In fact, my faith has grown stronger through these moments.

There is no way that we, on earth, can understand the wonders of heaven. I think that when people get into heaven the mysteries of our earthly life will all be revealed. Heaven, I am sure, is beyond our wildest dreams, which should make us all work a little harder to get there!

I believe that a person's faith is the most important factor of their life. It's necessary to attend Church often to be reminded of why we really are here- to love and serve our Lord! I believe that we will never be given tragedies, trials or adversities that we cannot handle. God will always give us the strength and grace to make it through every situation. Sometimes maybe the Lord pushes us here and there and it is up to us to work it out and to try to turn it into something good. The power of prayer can overcome all of our problems. Sometimes it just seems to take longer than we wish!

Appendix: History of the Reagan Name

The surname REGAN or REAGAN was derived in most cases from the Celtic Riagan or Riagain which means "kinglet", but other sources claim that it has been derived from the Irish Raighameaning "to biggit" (inhabit), and from Raigan, meaning "religious."

In ancient Irish and early American records the name appears in the various spellings of O'Riagain, O'Riagan, O'Reagain, O'Riaghan, O'Riaghain, O'Regaine, O'Riegaine, O'Regane, O'Regan, Riagan, Reagain, Reagin, Reagen, Regen, Ragon, Ragin, Ragan, Ragen, Ragins, Ragens, Reggon, Reagon, Reagan, Regan, and others. Of the forms mentioned, the last two are those most frequently in evidence in America in more recent times.

The O'Regans of Meath were a branch of the southeren Ui Neill and one of the four tribes of Tara. The heads of this line were lords of South Breagh, County Meath, and of the North of the present County of Dublin, prior to the time of the Anglo-Norman invasion of Ireland. They were a powerful family in that vicinity. They trace their descent from Raighan, son of Cineth, son of Flann Da Congall, a descendant of Heremon, one of the first Milesian Monarchs of Ireland. In the year 1029 A.D. Matgamain O'Riagain, King of Breagh, won a noble victory over Amhlaoibh, son of Sitric, King of Dublin. The members of the family were soon afterwards dispersed throughout Ireland and one branch became chiefs of Hy Riagain, now the Barony of Tinehinch, Queen's County, Ireland.

190

Dubhrean, son of Dubhgall, was the father of Dubhda, father of Maolcroine, whose son, Giollamuire Caoch O'Riaghain, was Chief of the Hy Raigain, Queen's County. Probably of the above-mentioned family were Maurice Regan, secretary to Dermod MacMurough, King of Leinster, and Sir Teigue or Teige O'Regan, a distinguished officer in the Irish army of King James II. Possibly, however, Maurice Regan of, Leinster, was descended from the O'Regans or Raigans who trace their descent from Cahir or Cathire More, King of Ireland A.D. 144, through his son, Rossa Failge. Some of the descendants of this clan possessed lands in the County of Cavan, but most of them resided in Leinster. Leinster is a former province in S.E. Ireland.

The O'Regans of Thomond are of a Dalcassian family, descended from Riagan, son of Donncuan or Donchuan, son of Cineadh, King of Thomond, and brother of Brian Boru, the one hundred and seventy-fifth Monarch of Ireland, who was born in the year 926. This line had its origin in Heber, son of Miled, another of the early Milesian Monarchs of Ireland.

Among the many later records of the name in Ireland are those of Dr. James O'Regan, of Mallow, County Cork, whose will was recorded in the year 1803; Thomas O'Regan, a grocer, of Mungret Street, Limerick, who married a daughter of Thady O'Halloran, of Ballyounnane, County Clare, in the year 1807; Thomas O'Regan, of Drogheda, whose will was recorded in 1811; Thomas Regan of Moygownagh, whose daughter, Mary, was married in the early nineteenth century to John O'Hart; and Mary Regan, who married Michael O'Murphy, of Kilbonane, in the Barony of Muscry, toward the end of the nineteenth century.

As early as the year 1668, one Daniel Ragan was living in Surry County, VA. In 1687 he and Francis Regan, probably a brother, were listed among the foot soldiers of that county. Nothing is definitely known of the immediate descendants of these early immigrants to America, but later records of the Virginia Colony mention Michael Regan Jr., of Fairfax County, in 1756; John Regan, of Frederick County, in 1758; and John Reagan, of Frederick County (probably identical with the preceding John), whose will was recorded in 1767.

Cornelius Regan, probably the progenitor of the family of the name in Maryland, died in Calvert County, MD., in 1673, but the names of his children, if any, are not in evidence. Among the probable descendants of this immigrant were Timothy Reagan, who witnessed the will of Richard Moss, of Anne Arundel County, MD., in 1700; Timothy Regan (probably identical with the last-mentioned Timothy), who witnessed the will of Nicholas Dorsey, of Baltimore County, in 1717; and Philip Reagan, of St. Mary's County, MD., whose will is dated 1718.

About the year 1729 several members of the ancient Irish family of O'Regan emigrated to Pennsylvania, where they dropped the prefix "O" from their name. James and Michael Reagan of Pennsylvania, who served in the War of the States, may have been descended from one of these immigrants, but the early records do not clearly show this. In 1790 seven of the name, James Reagin, Weldin Reagan, Reason Reagan, Stephen Regan, John Regan, George Ragon, and Philip Ragin, were listed as heads of families in the Pennsylvania census.

One branch of the Pennsylvania family of the name is believed to have settled at an early date in Guilford County, NC. In that state are found the records of John Reagan and his wife Mary, living in 1772, who were the parents of a daughter named Elizabeth and a son named James.

The son James married Nancy Cook and settled near Knoxville, TN., where he died in 1827. By an earlier wife (nee Hays), James was the father of a son named John, and by his second wife, Nancy, he had six children, James, Charles, Frances, Peter, William, and Rebekah. By a third wife, whose name is not known, James Sr., had three daughters, May, Ann, and Rachel.

John, eldest son of James Sr., had two children, James Hayes Reagan, of Sweetwater Valley, TN., and a daughter named Sarah. James, son of James Sr., removed to Georgia and was married in Elbert County in 1805 to Mary Dandridge Morrison, of that place. Their children were William Morrison, John, Martha, Nancy A., Charles, Joseph, James, Francis Washington, Mary Dandridge, Sarah Elizabeth, and Thomas Jefferson Reagan.

Of the last-mentioned brothers, Francis Washington, a doctor, made his home at Atlanta, GA.Peter, son of James Sr., married Nancy Cunnyngham or Cunningham, of Monroe County, TN., and removed with her to Rome, GA.; where he left at least two children, Carrie and Addie Reagan.

John or James H. Reagan, supposedly a cousin of the before-mentioned James Hayes Reagan, of Tennessee, became Postmaster General, Governor of Texas, and United States Senator fo Texas in the first half of the eighteenth century. However, the names of his progeny, if any, are not of record.

Timothy Reagan, a native of East Tennessee, was married before 1834 to Barbara Schultz, of German ancestory. To this union was born at least one son, Benjamin B. Reagan, and by a second wife, Martha Moore, Timothy had seven other children. Benjamin B. Reagan, son of the first union, removed with his parents to Madison County, MO., at an early age. He married Utica Kinkelman, of Missouri, in 1861 and had issue by her of three daughters, Edith B., Mary M., and Grace E.

Alexander C. Reagan, also of Tennessee, removed with his parents in the early nineteenth century to Alabama and thence to Mississippi. In that State he married Rhonda Wood, by whom he was the father of James W. and William Reagan. The father removed with his two sons to Texas about 1853, and the sons removed soon after his death to Louisiana.

Of these brothers, James W. married Amanda Stewart in 1869 and had issue by her of E. Brown, Alice, Lillie, and Augustus Reagan, of Louisiana; while William married Mary Frances Anderson in 1869. To this union were born six children, Mary Marguerite, Webb P., James W., Sallie L., Claude Douglas, and John W. Reagan, of Louisiana.Peter Reagan, possibly related to the above-mentioned Tennessee lines, was the father about the middle of the nineteenth century by his wife Nancy of a son named John, who married Nancy Finley and was the father by her of Joel L. Reagan, who married Lucy C. Beaty. To this union was born at least one son, James Blaine Reagan, of Fentress County, TN. Evidently of the same family were George W. Reagan and William Louis Reagan, of the same county.

In the early eighteenth century one Thomas Reagain, probably of Irish descent, settled in Cumberland County, NJ. His will, dated 1749, names four sons, Lazerus, Gaberall or Gabriel, Benjamin, and Nebucadnezer. Later records of the New Jersey lines of the family include those of Gabriel Reagain, of Cape May, who married Susannah Gaudy in 1749, and of Elizabeth Christina Regan, who married Simeon Vernor, of Somerset County, NJ, in 1767.

Another family of the name was seated about the middle of the eighteenth century in New York. The early records are not complete, but the will of John Rider, of Dutchess County, NY, dated 1774, mentions his grandchildren, Elenor, Hulda, and Thomas Regan.

Patrick Reagan, of Kansas, whose ancestry is not known, was the father in 1864 by his wife, Catherine Trayner, of a son named James William, who made his home in Missouri, Kansas, California, and other parts of the West and Southwest.

John Reagan, son of Charles Reagan, of Ireland, was born in that country in 1858 and came to America before 1883. In the last-mentioned year he married Rhoda Duffy, of St. Johnsbury, VT, and settled with her at Littleton, NH. His children were Mary, Charles, John, James, and Leo.Best known for their intellectual attainments, resourcefulness, and sound judgment, the Regans and Reagans of America have been successful as lawyers, educators, engineers, businessmen, architects, judges, and public officials. They have shown themselves possessed of imagination, sound business sense, the ability to lead and direct others, and often a keen sense of justice and right.

Among those of the name who served with the Colonial forces in the American Revolution were Captain Charles, Ensign Daniel, Denis, Phillip, Captain Richard, Thomas, and William Reagan or Regan, of Virginia; Bartholomew, Brice, and John Ragan, Ragen, Reagin, or Reagon, of Virginia; Darby, James, Morris, and Roderick Ragan or Regen, of Maryland; Bartholomew Reagon, of Maryland; James,John, and Michael Reagan, of Pennsylvania; William Regen, of Pennsylvania; Basil, Daniel, Francis, James, Michael, Thomas, and William Regan, of Pennsylvania;

Jerrit or Jerret Regin, of Pennsylvania; Thomas Reagon, of North Carolina; Charles, John, and Richard Regan, of North Carolina; Darby Reagan, of Georgia; and many more from the other States of that period.

(Compiled by THE MEDIA RESEARCH GROUP Washington, D.C.)

Bibliography

1. Constitutional Rights Foundation. Irish Immigration to the U.S. Bill of Rights in Action, Winter 2010 (Volume 26, No. 2).
2. O'Laughlin, Michael C. Mac, Mc, and O Names in Ireland, Scotland, & America, 2003.
3. Knopf, Michael. Grand Rapids History: Grand Rapids Streetcars, May 10, 2008.
4. Paul G.Goebel <http://en.wikipedia.org/wikiIWikipedia>
5. The History of Prohibition. Pivotal Events of the 1900s. <http://history1900s.about.com/od/1920s/p/prohibition.html>
6. The Great Depression. <**http://www.u-s-history.com**>
7. Century of Progress Exposition --Chicago World's Fair, 1933-1934. <http//.cityclicker.net/chicfair/>
8. The Bachelor's Children. History of Radio. <http://www.otrcat.com/bachelors-children>
9. Salk Institute for Biological Studies. <http://poliotoday/>
10. Taylor, Alan. *The Atlantic.* World War II: Pearl Harbor. JUL 31, 2011
11. Women in the Military during World War II.<http://www.mnhs.org>
12. The 6th Bomb Group. <http://philcrowther.com/6bgmain.html>
13. The Enola Gay and the 509th Composite Group
14. Greenberg, Milton. The GI Bill of Rights. U.S. Department of State, *Historians on America.*
15. Jones, Tim. *The Chicago Tribune* //www.chicagotribune.com/news/politics/chi-chicagodays-deweydefeats-story.
16. History of Television, History.com. www.history.com.
17. Fluoride in Drinking Water. http://grcity.us/enterprise-services/Water-System/Fluoride-in-Drinking-Water.aspx.
18. Glenner, Dr. Richard. *Journal of the History of Dentistry*, Vol. 48, No. 2. July,2000.
19. History of St. Mary's Parish. Pioneer Times. Centennial Ed., 1971.
20. 1964 New York World's Fair. <http://64nywf65.20m.com/>
21. Uses of Penicillin. <http://herbarium.usu.edu/penicillin/>
22. Friedlander Jr., Blaine. Former Smithsonian director lectures about Enola Gay controversy.
23. The History of Elderhostel, Inc. and Road Scholar <http://www.roadscholar.org/about/history.asp>

Family Reflections

Jane Ellen "Punie" Reagan

I am the oldest of the Reagan siblings so I had the luxury of having been an "only child" for all of eleven months before my sister was born! But some of my earliest memories involve trips:

- To Dad's folks', my Reagan grandparents' home, only 30 minutes away, in Grand Rapids for holidays. Their home was small and kind of dark. Dad's youngest brothers are only 10 years older than I am, so they often were expected to entertain us kids. Also, it seems we were to be seen and not heard, although we were not punished for speaking up, but expected to find other things to do while the grown-ups talked.

- I know we flew in once a year to Milwaukee to see my Mom's family—grandparents, aunts, uncles and cousins. I think Mom made a deal with Dad that if he was going to settle his dental practice far away from her family in another state, she wanted to visit her family at least once a year. I think he kept that promise and it worked out great. We got to spend precious time with even far-away grandparents.

- Trips in the car, even if they were to or from Grand Rapids, with the whole family, were a challenge, I'm sure.

- I do remember seeing and smelling my dad's occasional smoking pipe and cigars when he was home doing things around the yard or house, which was essentially weekends. I now know he didn't necessarily like doing yard work, but I remember the smell of freshly cut grass from our tiny lawn.

- Birthdays in our family are big deals. It's your one day of the year when you're special and get all the attention with a cake baked to your orders, and family dinner where everyone sings to you and you get to open your few modest presents. No matter what, the birthday celebrations occurred, with Mom as the organizer of these. We waited 'til Dad got home from the office to do this part of the celebrating.

Other things our family celebrated (then and now) are major holidays. While growing up, we'd go to Grandma and Grandpa Reagan's home for some of these—Christmas, Thanksgiving, Easter is what I'm talking about. Others we'd stay at our home, and as the family grew, it got harder to get everyone in one car to go anywhere! We still celebrate these holidays and when we got married, we were given the OK to be with our new family. So often when asked how many will be there, if I'm not hosting the event, I have no idea which of my siblings are coming until that day or when I arrive. Only the host of the get-together needs to know exactly who's coming and what dish they'll bring to share.

When we were sick, it was Mom who took care of us, cleaned us up, changed our pajamas and sheets, and expressed tremendous sympathy. Dad had a hard time dealing with vomit (!) so when it came to those awful accidents in the middle of the night Dad was not a part of that as far as I can remember; he mostly just stayed out of the way.

My dad shows me that God is first. Also, loyalty to one's spouse is very important. He taught us about community activism (giving back to the community or profession).

Because of his example, we have always been physically active. Golf, biking, going to the lake, snow skiing, etc. are fun things that keep you healthy. **All** of us of (his children and also  his grandchildren) are physically active and in very good shape, and much of that is Dad's credit, but mom gets credit for teaching us by example about healthy eating. Thank goodness we were not a junk food family.

I don't think Dad has changed much over time. He's a great storyteller and can spin a yarn with anyone, no matter where he is: on a ski chair lift, in line at the New York World's Fair. He has never been patient—HATES lines of people, cars, traffic jams, and will even leave an important football game at any level to avoid delays in getting out of the parking lot. When driving, he'd rather pull out in front of a car than be more cautious and wait for it to pass. His impatience has remained the same or increased!

Dad has definitely learned from his grandkids how important it is to spend time with young children. He often talks about his regret that he didn't spend more time with us, his children, but we have no hang-ups about it.

Grandfriends Day, Ada Christian School, 2009.

I admire Dad's ability to focus on what's going on now; he's a guy who is generally "in the moment" and engages with people around him. He did this with his dental patients (and I saw that as I worked for him while in high school); with his friends at Euchre Club (I think it was 8 couples who got together once a month for 50 years!); with his social friends at St. Patrick's Day; with watching sports and praying.

Dad is a relatively easy-going guy and rarely did I see him enraged, so that's a trait —our generally laid back personalities—that almost every one of us has, modeled by both Dad and our Mom.

Dad loves recording events, on either family movies or his scrapbooks. He is not a good writer, so these are his modes of recording almost all major events and activities of the family for essentially the past 60 years. We are

 thrilled that some of these family movies will be converted to digital modes and able to share with anyone anytime (until the technology changes again, of course!).

I appreciate that Dad knows how to have a good time. He loves to laugh, hear good stories, travel, explore new foods, restaurants, destinations, and while there, learn about the topic/area. He's curious and not afraid to ask or get more information.

Dad liked the idea of an annual family vacation, starting a little over 50 years ago. If it were up to Mom, we'd have stayed home. So because of his initiative, we saw some wonderful parts of the United States, camped, fished (a little) and had some very memorable vacations together.

Karen, Bob and Jane, Columbia River Gorge, Oregon, 2009.

Dad's favorite movie is "The Sound of Music." He likes traditional Irish songs like *Danny Boy* and *When Irish Eyes Are Smiling*.

He found a poster that reinforced a huge part of our lives growing up: each child had jobs to do around the house from the time they were able, like 5-6 years old. The poster was huge—like 6 feet wide and 5 feet tall, and it was mounted on our kitchen wall above hooks that held our portable recipe-card-containing jobs for that week. Certain age groups rotated those jobs. The poster said in huge black letters: **YOU MUST KNOW YOUR JOB AND DO IT!!!** Our friends, and anyone who came to our house through the back door, saw that sign and commented on it. He generally reinforced Mom's rules for all of us, and that was one of the most overt signs of his support!

Dad is famous for NOT being a first-class dresser. His frugality, a.k.a cheapness, shows in his casual clothing, mostly in the summer when it's hot. He has worn the exact same shorts and shirt (that are horribly put together) to the Reagan family reunion for the past 10 years at least. It's a family joke how bad his clothes are!

He loved trying to be handy. For family vacations, he built several wooden luggage carriers to mount on top of the station wagon, and projects like that were his pride and joy. He was always working on some remodel job in the house, and let's say he was not a master carpenter, but he was real creative and all his work resulted in improvements, and often very functional things like drawers, additional shelves, an additional closet, aski rack, a Christmas/Easter/St.Patrick's Day sign mounted on the front porch roof...All designed, made, painted and mounted by him.

Dad's soft spot for his grandkids is blatantly obvious. He's never said it that I remember, but his actions embody the phrase we hear often: "If I'd known how much fun grandkids were, I'd have had them first!" He loves being around those grandkids, especially when they're small, like before 10 years old. He loves teasing them as they get verbal, and challenging them with kidding and joking around.

I am proud to see my siblings sharing their families with Dad in an amazing way. Every single one of my siblings who has children lives within 15 minutes of Dad. That is no accident, in my observation. They knew raising their children in a small, safe community like the one they grew up in would allow them to raise children in a loving environment like they experienced.

They are also able to spend lots of time together- the siblings, spouses, 23 cousins, and now their spouses and friends are all able to share good times, support each other in bad times, and keep in touch. This means that the positive, loving environment created by my Mom and Dad can't help but live on! Dad loved my mother deeply and thoroughly. He feels guilty now for not being perfect with her, but that's simply being human— NO ONE appreciates what they have 'til it's gone. He went to work every day and provided a good life for his family. He encouraged us all to go to college or otherwise do something to assure our independence.

Dad taught us by example and in practice to appreciate what we have and to work for what we want. There was no assumption of entitlement in our family. You were entitled to get a set of luggage when you graduated from high school (all of us!) and get out there and make something of yourself!! Also, none of us ever received a car for a gift. We were all expected to pay our own way for college, which forced us to make careful strategic decisions once we turned 18. Those lessons all have helped us be stronger, smarter adults.

Karen Elizabeth "Keren" Reagan Myers
Daughters: Emily, Colleen, Lorri and Becky

One of the memories that I have about Dad from my childhood is wrestling with him after dinner on the floor in the living room. Also, I remember combing his hair while sitting on his shoulders as he read the evening GR Press.

Karen Myers and her proud father celebrate her BSN in 2008!

I remember tobogganing at Bertha Brock Park on Sundays with Dad in the winter and beating all the others, as we had the most people on ours! Dad was always up for an adventure: vacationing to Yellowstone National Park, The World's Fair in New York City and also held in Montreal, Canada.

We enjoyed ice skating on the rink he made in the back yard, and sometimes Dad would take us to the rink at the cement building by the pool. I remember riding the Little Train and having ice cream afterwards in the summer and sneaking into the Showboat every night during its week run in July.

Peg, Karen and Dad in Ireland,

Birthdays were usually celebrated at home with our siblings. I recall being able to choose the color of frosting as a special treat and opening lots of presents, too.

Sometimes we had friends over and played "Button, button, who's got the button?", dropped clothespins into the jar, and played pin the tail on the donkey, etc.

A lesson that I learned from Dad is that it is important to work hard and give back to your community. Family ties are important, as are God and church and our religion. Dad showed us that having sense of humor helps...so does knowing the phone numbers of tradesmen for the difficult home repair projects.

Dad's stamina and energy level, for his age, are remarkable, even after rounds of chemotherapy.   Since 2007, the change in being alone without his spouse is also evident. He is much more emotional and vulnerable, in my opinion.

I admire Dad's commitment to his family, God, the community, friends and neighbors. I admire his love for being outside and being physically fit. He is willing to try new things, go to new places, and allow his daughters to accompany him on outings and trips. He can effortlessly ease into conversations and can fit into any situation or setting.

Bob and Karen in Lourdes, France, 2011.

Dad's favorite songs, phrases and sayings are pretty predictable because they are anything Irish and Catholic. His favorite things usually fall under the themes of dentistry and golf.

Karen's housewarming party.

Dad loves making scrapbooks and displaying any or all items in his possession (rather crudely, too I must admit!). He is an Irish Catholic family man, which makes him endearing.

I want my children to know that Dad (pictured with Mom and Emily, 2006) is a man of strength, character, wit, humility, piety and spirit.

My father has also loved his family, but sometimes had difficulty showing his love, as many men did in the past. He speaks his mind, bluntly at times, too.

I know my dad loves me in his actions, deeds, and ability to listen and give advice when asked.

Kathleen Elaine "Kuee" Reagan Ormiston
Husband: Jim Ormiston
Children: Tara and Evan

I am the third-born daughter and the ONLY child with blond hair and blue eyes. I have been teased that my dad was the milkman, even to this day. It must be that I take after my mom's side of the family since Grandma Callan's sister had blue eyes.

I remember Dad coming home after work every day, sitting in his favorite chair in the living room, and all of us kids taking turns sitting on his shoulders combing his (thinning) hair while he read the paper. He put a lot of 'stuff' in his hair, so it was fun to play with because it stood straight up.

Dad came home from work every day for lunch. When I was in junior high, I, too, came home for lunch because school was only three blocks away. Though I don't recall eating lunch with him, I do recall that he shaved at lunchtime in the bathroom near the kitchen.

We went on fabulous family vacations every summer. Many times we went with the Doyle family and camped. My favorite memories of all these vacations are when we stopped at the rest areas and we had lunch.

When I was in 7th or 8th grade I remember that Dad had season tickets to the MSU football games. He would take one of us with him...I always wanted him to pick me. I'm not sure how this could happen, but I remember Dad and I sitting in the back seat of the car on the way home (no idea who was driving); I laid my head on his shoulder to take a nap.

I also remember watching sports with him every Sunday in the sunroom. I watched golf, baseball (Tigers) and football with him. When I was 11 years old, the catcher of the Tigers was Bill Freehan, and he was number 11, too. I thought that was so cool. I think these Sundays gave me my love (to this day) of sports. I love love love watching football. One of the MSU games that Dad took me to, I had to have been either 15 or 16 because he handed me the keys on the way to the car (after the game) and told me to drive.....I was VERY surprised and nervous, but I got us home.

I worked for my dad at his dental office during high school. He was very patient in teaching me how to assist him chair-side. I loved it and I think I was very good at it. I went on to Ferris University for Dental Assisting. (Unfortunately, all I did was party at school...dad knows this).

The Reagans at the Ormiston pool.

I was the first child to get married and I recall on the way to the church, the morning of my wedding, Mom and Dad drove me, so it was just the three of us. They both talked to me about the sacrament I was about to receive and how important it was to uphold the vow. They asked me if I was SURE...which I know now, they were giving me the option to back out if I wasn't sure.

Dad was and is a good provider for his family. He is a rock solid example of the responsibilities a (traditional) man has in the household. He never lectured, and he actually is a man of few words. This may be due to the fact that there were soooooooooo many females in the house and he never got a chance to talk. But, when he did have something to say, we all listened.

Dad outwardly loved our mom. He showed he loved her and we all witnessed it. I don't recall him ever saying anything bad or negative about any of the boys I dated. He really never said (or says) anything negative, ever. I believe his work ethic rubbed off on all of us. Most of us had the chance to work for him during high school. We also saw our dad go off to work every day. When we worked for him, we HAD to be on time, we HAD to put in a full day of 'work'...versus just showing up.

I know that we are all very proud of our father and his dedication to his profession, his love of life-long learning, his passion for golf, his love of our mom, his ability to be patient and kind, his willingness to let us learn through our own mistakes, his resilience in handling tragedy (our sister's death) and watching his children go through sorrow and loss (two sisters are divorced). I am who I am because of the balanced upbringing I had. My dad was the rock. My mom was the emotional support. I love my dad with my whole heart and soul AND I know he knows it.

James Edward Reagan
Wife: Becky
Children: Jacob, Tess and Judi

Jim, Tess, Judi, Becky and Jacob Reagan at Niagra Falls.

When we celebrated birthdays, since we had 10 kids we always had a party if even half the family showed up. Dad always had the movie camera and later the VCR to record the blowing out of the candles with everyone at the table. So, in the footage for birthday celebrations, the cameraman (Dad) was conspicuously absent. After dinner we would have the birthday cake for desert. We would all line up for the "spanking machine," and the birthday subject had to run the gauntlet, scampering on all fours between everyone's legs. We did that for years until the subject seemed to be too big to go between the youngest kids' legs.

Since we had a nurse for a mom, she took our temperature when we were sick. We knew when dad was sick because he would put on his pajamas.

He probably only had to wear his pajamas once every 5 or 10 years.

Dad instilled in us to respect our parents. He did not like it when we talked back to him or Mom. It was obvious that he respected and admired our mother. If our parents did argue they did not do it in front of us. These days when I see a husband disrespect, hit or abuse his wife on TV or in a movie, or when I witness this kind of behavior among acquaintances, it is unacceptable to me. I learned from my dad that women should be respected, and I have tried to emulate that as a husband myself.

Dad has a creative streak and was always the family artist; he could draw almost anything. He helped create the "Know Your Job & Do It" poster, which listed our chores.

Jim and Bob Reagan, Ireland, 2008.

I think that Dad has mellowed over time. With children at home always testing parental limits, he had to be strict and he set rules, curfews, and behavior limits. After we left home he did not have to be strict, which was probably a relief.

We watched many Lions football games, and during halftime we would play catch with a softball and baseball. Our yard was too small to play a baseball game. He always made time to play a round of golf, and I only could beat him when he played really poorly and I played really well.

One thing that I admire about Dad is that it was very obvious that he enjoyed his work as a dentist. As I have learned, It is very precise detail work, and you must be able to focus. He rarely missed work because he was rarely sick. He liked to whistle, and before dental masks became common he whistled at work. Some old patients ask me why I don't whistle like he did.

One tradition that we had as a family was that Dad cooked hotdogs every Sunday night on the gas Charmglow grill. Many Sunday evenings we would watch golf on TV and then have hotdogs in the sunroom. We would all watch *The Ed Sullivan Show* on Sunday if golf was not on. Later we'd watch *All in the Family* and *M.A.S.H.* He also used to watch *McHales Navy* with Ernest Borgnine.

Dad has always liked a good golf game. As he got older, the younger/stronger guys that he played against would sometimes beat him. Mom could always tell how Dad had played by how hard he slammed the car door shut when he would return. He did not like to hit a bucket of balls on the range, but went right to the 1st tee as quickly as possible. My job when I got into mischief was to clean all the dried-up grass that was stuck to his golf balls.

Father's Day 2000: Jim and Evan Ormiston, Ed and Jake Reagan, Bob Reagan, Rich and Cole Wade.

Dad has shown his love by being there for all 10 of his kids. He worked long days at the office to support our family. He would take Thursday afternoons off to golf in the summer, and I am thankful that he took us on family vacations and ski trips. He set the example of being faithful, caring and loving to our mother. Dad also gave us the example of being a good Catholic; he did not just tell us what a good Catholic should do, but he has lived it.

Because of Dad, I know that it is important to be civic minded. It is important for him to be part of the solution if there was a problem. He was very active in organizations, and he truly liked people!

One way that he showed how much he enjoyed people was when he and Mom threw a big St. Patrick's Day party every year. Lots of people would show up. Mom would start the singing with her choir friends from church, and Dad would keep the punch bowl filled and spiked. Lots of us kids were the servers, and our job was to keep the food bowls filled; we always had lots and lots of Jumbo shrimp. Nobody ever left without having a grand time.

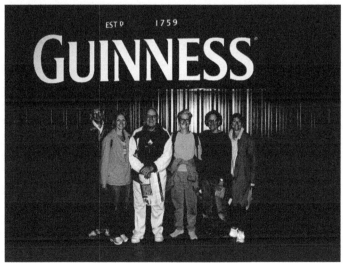

Guinness Brewery, Ireland: Jim, Kuee, Dad, Punie, Keren, and Peg, 2008.

Margaret (Peggy) Erin "B" Reagan LaPenna
Husband: Bill LaPenna
Children: Joey, Frankie and Vinnie

One of my earliest memories of Dad was that he would come home from work on his bike, fix himself a drink, and then sit in the living room and read the newspaper. I would sit on his shoulders and comb his hair while he was reading the newspaper. I know it sounds kind of crazy but we just loved to do that.

Another memory is that we always went on fantastic family vacations in the summer. One of my favorites was to Yellowstone National Park. Dad would drive the motorhome, and while he was driving we would be standing in the motorhome making bologna sandwiches. When we would get to the next rest stop we would pull over, get out and eat the bologna sandwiches.

Another favorite vacation was we went to Expo 67 in Montreal, Canada with the Doyle family. We went on many, many summer vacations with the Doyle family. One of the funniest things I remember, and we have family movies to back this up, is we pulled over at some park and Jim Reagan and Brian and Kevin Doyle had to go to the bathroom in the woods. The girls (Karen Doyle and Mary and me, and maybe Ruth) would chase after them like we wanted to follow them into the woods. They would turn around and chase us, and then we would chase them, and Dad got all of this on film and it's absolutely hysterical to watch.

Another memory of Expo 67 is when we went to a Chinese restaurant (five Doyle kids and probably eight Reagan kids, plus the four adults) and the waitresses kept refilling our water glasses. We would take a sip and they would come over immediately and refill our water glass. Then we all started giggling and laughing hysterically because as soon as we would drink our water they would refill it, until finally we turned to Mom and said, "Do we HAVE to keep drinking all this water?" We thought we had to drink it.

Another fond memory is when we spent holidays with the Doyle family. We'd go over to their house every Memorial Day, Fourth of July and Labor Day and have a cookout: hamburgers, hotdogs and probably the adults had steaks. I remember we pretty much would have the run of the house and could do whatever we wanted as long as we left the adults alone. We would go into the basement and make prank phone calls.

I worked in Dad's office when I was a senior in high school. It was a really good experience getting to know Dad as a boss. It was different, and it was a new experience looking at him as a boss and not as a dad.

04/26/2009

Bill and Vinnie LaPenna, Bob Reagan: Vinnie's 1st Holy Communion, 2009.

I think my strongest sentiment about my dad is how lucky I was to be in a family with two loving parents. Yes, they were very strict, but looking back now, it was in a good way. We siblings have often talked about how Mom and Dad never ever, ever, ever fought. And even after we were older we used to ask, "Did you fight?" They always said they didn't. So it's kind of tough in your own marriage to try to live up to their perfect standard.

I think what Mom and Dad should be most proud of with us kids is that ten kids and their spouses all get along. We all show up for Christmas and Thanksgiving, and there's never any bad feelings or bad vibes. That we all like each other is a testament to what excellent parents they were. And I would say the secret to that is the old saying: a family that prays together, stays together.

Dad and Joey.

Dad, Mom and Frankie.

Dad and Vinnie.

Punie, Pit, Dad, Peg (pregnant with Frankie), Ruth, Kuee.

Ruth Ann "Rudy" Thomet
Husband: Steve Thomet
Children: Caroline, Sam, Spencer and Annie

Fond memories with my dad include those fall days watching football games on Saturdays and Sundays, and watching M*A*S*H, Bob Hope specials and eating popcorn. Some activities we enjoyed at the OCHC cabin were: beach days in Pentwater, playing euchre and horseback riding. While dad certainly did not ride, he enjoyed taking us and picking us up so he could chat with the owner (who was dirt poor but horse rich) and give him a nice tip.

I am thankful that Dad taught me to ski. I remember one trying time up the bunny hill towrope. My skis were in a tangle, and it felt as though my legs were twisted around each other four or five times.

Try as I might, I couldn't get straightened out, and I was holding up the towrope. Dad's strong arms picked me up high enough so that my legs dangled beneath me to straighten out, and up we went!

We enjoyed yearly vacations in Northern Michigan to ski and then later out West. My ski trip memories include the tired satisfaction that we felt after a day of skiing and sitting around that evening talking about the events of the day: our favorite run, who had the most spectacular fall, etc.

The Reagan family in front of the King Street house, October 12, 2007.

Dad was always busy with something. He undertook many carpentry projects, and there were always good smells in his basement workshop (even his cigar). I remember the sound of him whistling while he worked.

When we were small, it was a thrill to ride on Dad's shoulders to the dinner table. Afterwards, he would play football with us in the living room. To level the playing field, he would be on his knees, but he still towered over us as we tried to make a touchdown. The goals were the fireplace and the hallway.

Dad has mellowed over time. For example, he doesn't *always* have to be ahead of everyone else when driving a car!

I admire his quiet leadership ability and his great faith. I admire his giving nature; he was always generous with his family, his community and his church.

I have learned many lessons from my dad:

•the importance of professional involvement and giving back to the community

•the importance of admitting your mistakes

•the importance of <u>telling</u> your spouse that you love him/her. Dad experienced profound grief after our mom died in that he felt he did not verbally tell her how much she meant to him before she died. So deep was this regret that some time after her death he called his children together for a "family meeting." The sole purpose of the meeting, the only message he wanted to relay to us was: Tell your spouse you love him/her.

•to keep busy. He was always "doing" and very seldom idle.

Dad's sense of humor is always enjoyable. He delights in telling a good story or joke, as evidenced by the twinkle in his eye while delivering the story/joke.

He whistled all the time, especially while working, whether it was in his dental office, workshop or on a project. He has always loved popcorn and warm beer.

Dad invented the **"YOU MUST KNOW YOUR JOB AND DO IT"** poster to instill in us a sense of responsibility.

I would like my children and grandchildren to know that Dad enjoyed his dental work and is loved by his fellow professionals and community members. I would also like them to know that he loved his wife, their grandmother.

After my sister's death, Mom was going through the great difficulty of losing a child and we kids were not being as sensitive to her as we should have been. Dad called a meeting with maybe three or four of us older kids and gave us a VERY stern, frank talk about our selfish behavior and our need to be more kind and loving to our mother, his wife. He could see her anguish; we needed his stern lecture on our need to change our ways.

My father showed me that he loved me by making sure that the family spent time together, on vacations and at home. He instilled the practice of kneeling down for our daily Rosary. He always did what a dad is supposed to do: support his ever-growing family and always trusting that God would provide.

Patricia (Patty) Marie "Pit" Wade
Husband: Rich Wade
Children: Marie, Stephi, Cole, Erin, Lucy, Molly and
Melanie

One of my fondest memories is Dad taking us (Ruth, Patty, Don and Ed) out west skiing! We went without Mom because we were older and I'm sure she enjoyed the quiet house. I still love to downhill ski. Dad taught us all how to ski and we went often... the last few kids were pretty good skiers!

Christmas 2005, Molly and Melanie with Grandma and Grandpa Reagan.

Dad didn't like crowds so on Thursdays, his day off he would sometimes pick us up from St. Mary's elementary school and take us out to Cannonsburg. We also went up north to Boyne and Sugar Loaf often for a long weekend. Again, he didn't like to ski on the busy weekends so we'd go up for a few nights during the week. I remember staying in his friend's condo. Mom would make chili and we could ski right from the condo!!!

When someone had a birthday in our home we celebrated with a family dinner and angel food cake with whatever colored frosting we wanted! Lots of pictures would be taken and then we'd have to endure the dreaded "Spanking Machine." We had to crawl on all fours through our siblings' straddled legs to be spanked.

One lesson that I've learned from my dad is that hard work pays off.

Dad LOVES his grandkids, especially the little ones. When HE was younger and able he would get on all fours and let the grandkids pile on him, ride the horsie, etc.... I don't remember doing that as his daughter but LOVED seeing it with the grandkids.

Dad is God fearing. He was devoted to his wife and kids. He had other dentist friends that worked more hours, and had more toys and money. He worked but loved to PLAY whether it was golf, skiing or family vacations. He loves life and I enjoy his sense of humor.

I remember that Dad had an OLD bathrobe. I was in high school sitting at the kitchen table on a cold fall night with three girlfriends at about 10:00 on a Saturday night. Dad had been in the hot tub with a glass of wine. He stopped in the kitchen to say hi to us, then walked away towards the stairs to go to bed. As he walked away the four of us started LAUGHING hysterically out loud.......he had a HUGE hole in the back of his bathrobe. I was soooo thankful that he had his suit on!!!!!! My girlfriends & I still talk and laugh about that night like it was yesterday!!!!! He has a hard time getting rid of something until it is literally falling apart!!!

It's a family tradition to get together on December 22 to celebrate Mom's birthday. We meet at the cemetery, then get together for pizza and sledding.

Dad also comes over to do laundry at our house. He had a pair of jeans that we couldn't get him to replace, so one day I simply threw his old dingy jeans in the trash. When he came back to pick up his laundry a brand new pair of jeans came out of the dryer with his load of laundry!!!

I know Dad loves me because he remained faithful to his wife, he was active in the community to support the schools and businesses where we lived, he took us on vacations, skiing. During the holidays he would put an enormous pumpkin on the front porch roof!!! It's the little things he did for us that showed us his love. He has a hard time saying it but I know he loves us!!!

Donald Charles "Doon" Reagan
Wife: Michelle

Some of my earliest childhood memories are of you and Mom listening to my bedtime prayers. I'm not sure why that is, I just remember you sitting on the edge of my bed listening to nightly prayers. I knew at an early age that God and religion were important, and that it was to be taken seriously. I still remember the cowboy wallpaper and the three-bed assembly that you built for the boys' room with the train set that was set up to run around the top of the room.

One particular memory I have is a day that you and Mom got me out of school – in the middle of the morning! I must have been 7 or 8 years old and I couldn't figure out why you were there. I wasn't sick – I didn't remember getting on the nuns' nerves that morning more than usual that day. We got into the car and you surprised me with a trip to the circus downtown Grand Rapids! Cotton candy, lions, tigers, bears, elephants, clowns, trapeze artists, etc...I'm sure you did that with my brothers and sisters, but that day it was just the three of us and boy did I feel special. What a great memory!

Bob, Michelle, Jane and Don Reagan.

I remember as a child when you would come home from work for lunch or at the end of the day and you would acknowledge Mom with a "Hello Poopsie" or some other cute phrase along with a big smooch. I know that it didn't register to me at the time – but looking back, I realize that I do that same thing with Michele now! I always knew that you loved and honored Mom, and I feel that you helped pass that down to me to make sure to always make Michele feel honored, loved, and special.

I know that particularly the last months of Mom's life when you cared for her were difficult, but you handled it with love and compassion and I hope that if that time comes for me to look after someone I love that I can handle it as well as you did. I also remember when you came home from a long day at work and sat down to read the paper – and you let us kids climb all over you and "comb and style" your hair! I know that was probably the last thing you needed at the end of your day. As an adult working long days myself, looking back, you handled it with love and patience...More patience than I would have had!

Our family trips- Yellowstone, Boston, Grand Canyon, Badlands, Mount Rushmore, and weekends up to the cabin are great memories. I know that dragging 5 or more kids fighting and arguing about who is sitting on "my side" and "who is touching me" in an RV or station wagon might not have been much of a vacation for you and Mom, but I have great memories and experiences to look back on.

I especially loved the times we spent riding the mini-bikes around the old St. Mary's playground and up at the cabin. It gave us a bit of freedom and adventure exploring the 100+ acres in Ferry. Fishing, riding horses, riding the dunes, swimming....what great adventures we had.

We had some great skiing trips up north and especially out West. You and Mom did a great job exposing us to the outdoors, fun exercise, and fun family time together, though you did give Patty, Ed, and I a scare when you thought you were having a heart attack on the ski trip in Colorado!

Quite often you were busy with something in your basement wood shop building something or fixing something that we (ok – probably me) had broken...smoking your pipe – or King Edward cigars. I still believe that is why I love the smell of cigars and pipe tobacco. I remember when you let us "pretend" to smoke your pipes – while we "helped."

I remember playing dentist with your old dental drill set that you brought home. I bet there are still a couple hundred small drill holes in the workbench. You always made time for us and made us feel that we contributed to your projects instead of making us feel that we were in your way. I believe that has given me the confidence in my own life to fix things – repair, paint, and assemble, rather than always hiring someone else to do it. Installing your first hot tub was just one small example of your determination to "do it yourself" that I have admired and that you've passed down to us all.

Our family celebrations of birthdays – Easter, 4th of July, Thanksgiving, Christmas, etc... were always great (in quantity and quality) gatherings of family and friends. I always felt special on my birthdays and Christmas and that I was the center of attention. It wasn't until I was older and started dating and invited someone from the "outside" that I realized what an undertaking these events really were! Boy, did I get some wild-eyed looks and reactions from some of them!

I also remember you attending all the softball, baseball, basketball, football, etc.....games I had. With your dental, Lions Club, school board, etc....meetings, I still do not know where you found the time and energy to drag the lawn chairs and coolers to all those games!

You and Mom did a wonderful job of supporting our activities and it was always nice to look out into the crowd and know that you were there supporting us, win or lose. You taught us about playing fair, gamesmanship, playing as a team, win or lose as long as you tried your best. Today I see so many kids (and even adults my own age) that do not have these skills and discipline, and I thank you for teaching and instilling them in me. I also want to thank you for passing on your love of golf; is a huge part of my extra-curricular activities! Michele might say that it is too much of my life! It helped me get the great job I have today, as I met my boss on the golf course. I've been to some of the most beautiful places in the USA because of my love of golf.

I remember practicing in the 4H fairground hitting balls so we could win the hole-in-one contest down by the Grand River in GR. I have especially enjoyed our times together on the golf courses over the last 40+ years, and I thank you.

I know I should also acknowledge the sleepless / restless nights I'm sure I caused you and Mom over the years. I know that I was not always easy to love and understand. I know that I have made many stupid, selfish, and inconsiderate choices. I'm sure you had discussions about many of my shortcomings as a child and as an adult. For those times of pain and worry, I am truly sorry.

I have always been very proud to be a Reagan. When I look back on it now, it was always reassuring and strangely comforting when someone would look at me and say, "You're Doc Reagan's' son, aren't you?" Growing up in a town where everyone knows your dad, and the great accomplishments he has had professionally, in service to others, and raising 10 children was truly a great blessing.

I think every child grows up and wants to know that they are loved and that their parents are proud of them. I have always felt loved and I hope that I have made you proud of me, of the man and husband that I have become. I want you to know that I love you very much and am very proud to call you Dad.

246

Edward John "Bubba" Reagan
Wife: Colleen

I can remember looking forward to my Dad waking up from his post-work nap so that we could wrestle. Sometimes he would hold a penny in his hand, and if I could pry the penny out of his hand then I got to keep the penny. (Big spender!)

We did lots of skiing in Colorado and in Michigan. In Michigan it was typically at Cannonsburg. We did take vacations up to Sugar Loaf Resort each winter as well. One time when I was pretty little we went up to Chrystal Mountain. The line for the T-Bar was massive, and I don't know why we were riding this particular lift, as I had never ridden a T-Bar. I told my Dad that I didn't know how to "ride it," but he insisted we take the T-Bar and told me, "All you do is stand and let it pull you up the hill." After trying 3-4 times to "stand there and let it pull you up the hill" he decided to take the chair lift.

I remember when Dad got rushed to the hospital with chest pains on a ski vacation in Colorado while we were at Snowmass Ski Area. He had face-planted earlier that day with a ginormous video camera strapped to his chest, and had bruised the muscles deep in his chest. Hence, he thought he was having a heart attack.

With every trip to Colorado the altitude affected him more and more. On the first trip it didn't affect him until we were at the top of the ski area. On the second trip it affected him when we got to the hotel at the mountain. On the third trip it was when we approached the ski area, and on the fourth trip it was when the plane landed in Denver before the plane de-pressurized.

When Dad would get home from golfing on Thursday evenings we would typically be eating dinner. Judging by the loudness of the door either shutting or slamming, Mom would instruct us whether to be silent or if we could speak to him. Silence was much more common than speaking.

If there were two products and both did the same job, he would invariably choose the cheaper of the two, even if that meant replacing the cheaper item after a year and a half (hence the reason it was cheaper). Why buy a new lawnmower when we can buy this one from the side of this guy's garage that he rebuilt? This lawnmower would never start with less than 852 pulls and had a blade that couldn't cut a soft stick of butter.

I remember racing Dad home on bicycles from his office when I was young. Many years later, I threw up on him and the fill-in dental assistant when Dad had me lying horizontal in the dental chair. The impression material in my mouth was dripping down my throat, and I tried to sit up to alleviate the disgusting taste, and was pushed back down so as not to "disrupt" the impression making sequence. After two or three times of trying to sit up and being told not to and or being pushed back down, I was finally allowed to sit up when I vomited all over Dad and the temporary assistant.

Irish Proverbs

There's no fireside like your own fireside.

Never bolt the door with a boiled carrot.

What butter and whiskey will not cure, there is no cure for.

If a cat had a dowry, she would often be kissed.

To the raven her own chick is white.

A man loves his sweetheart the most, his wife the best, his mother the longest.

If you dig a grave for others, you might fall into it yourself.

Drink is the curse of the land. It makes you fight with your neighbor. It makes you shoot at your landlord and it makes you miss him.

Hunger is the best sauce.

Only the rich can afford compassion.

Listen to the sound of the river and you will get a trout.

May you live as long as you want, and never want as long as you live.

Time is a great story teller.

A friend's eye is a good mirror.

Good as drink is, it ends in thirst.

As the big hound is, so will the pup be.

Put silk on a goat, and it's still a goat.

Two shorten the road.

Made in the USA
Middletown, DE
25 April 2024

53456134R10146